Leadership Vs. Management

Leadership, Volume 1

Mowgli J. Bear

Published by Tritch Publishing Co., 2023.

While every precaution has been taken in the preparation of this book, the publisher assumes no responsibility for errors or omissions, or for damages resulting from the use of the information contained herein.

LEADERSHIP VS. MANAGEMENT

First edition. September 12, 2023.

Copyright © 2023 Mowgli J. Bear.

ISBN: 979-8985080605

Written by Mowgli J. Bear.

Table of Contents

Introduction 1

Chapter 1: Management vs. Leadership 8

Chapter 2: What Does it Take to Be a Good Leader 16

Be Authentic 19

Leading by Example 24

Routines 28

Attitude Gives Altitude 34

Working Towards a Goal 39

Decision Making 46

Chapter 3: What Good Leaders Look For 50

Defining Teams and Teamwork 51

Dealing with Dysfunctional Teams 52

Attributes of a Team Player 56

Why Teams Fail 59

Chapter 4: Training and Empowerment 61

Improving Your Own Skill Set 63

Improving Your Team So They Can Replace You 68

Chapter 5: Getting the Work Done: Problem Solving ... 73

Chapter 6: Sheep vs. Shepherd: Creating Value in Your Organization 81

Conclusion 90

References 93

To all of my teachers along the way both in the classroom and where the rubber meets the road. The lessons I've learned and real-world experience I've gained are invaluable, both as a leader and as a human being trying to make the world a little bit better and a little bit brighter. This book would not have the magic and movement that I feel so deeply in my soul without your guidance, even if it didn't feel like guidance at the time.

I am forever grateful for all you've taught and continue to teach me in this ever-changing world we share.

Management vs. Leadership

Make Your Business Culture Successful, Maintain Growth, and Retain People Even During Times of Crisis

Mowgli J. Bear

© **Copyright 2021 - All rights reserved.**

The content contained within this book may not be reproduced, duplicated, or transmitted without direct written permission from the author or the publisher.

Under no circumstances will any blame or legal responsibility be held against the publisher, or author, for any damages, reparation, or monetary loss due to the information contained within this book, either directly or indirectly.

Legal Notice:

This book is copyright protected. It is only for personal use. You cannot amend, distribute, sell, use, quote, or paraphrase any part, or the content within this book, without the consent of the author or publisher.

Disclaimer Notice:

Please note the information contained within this document is for educational and entertainment purposes only. All effort has been executed to present accurate, up-to-date, reliable, complete information. No warranties of any kind are declared or implied. Readers acknowledge that the author is not engaged in the rendering of legal, financial, medical, or professional advice. The content within this book has been derived from various sources. Please consult a licensed professional before attempting any techniques outlined in this book.

By reading this document, the reader agrees that under no circumstances is the author responsible for any losses, direct or indirect, that are incurred as a result of the use of the information contained within this document, including, but not limited to, errors, omissions, or inaccuracies.

Book Description

When seas become rough, the crew needs a good captain at the helm of the boat. The better the captain, the better the team! When it comes to leadership, the same principles apply; a team will weather any storm if they are led instead of managed. Unearthing your leadership abilities is critical in making your leadership journey a success. This book is for anyone in or considering a leadership role, whether a veteran or brand new to the game, who wants to unlock their true leadership potential—for the greater good of the team, their organization, and themselves.

Introduction

The aim of leadership should be to improve the performance of man and machine, to improve quality, to increase output, and simultaneously to bring pride of workmanship to people. Put in a negative way, the aim of leadership is not merely to find and record failures of men but to reduce the causes of failure; to help people do a better job with less effort.

W. Edwards Deming

You have finally made it to the proverbial corner office. You have your own team. You might even have an expense account and a secretary. You are now in the big leagues—whoop de freakin' do. Now stop patting yourself on the back, because I'm here to give you a reality check.

You might have the word manager in your job title now, but that means you are now the least important person, with the most responsibility, to walk into the room. Remember the timeless adage: "Great power brings great responsibility." If you want to be the best manager for your team, forget about the power and focus your energy on your people and the responsibilities that have been given to you.

The moment you became a manager, you should have removed "me" from your vocabulary and replace it with "we." You no longer exist as a single entity but as a collective. Now your main focus should be on how you'll get the best from your people, processes, and equipment. You'll be doing this for the greater good of the people you're leading, the organization you work in, and the communities you support...it's time to step up your game.

> *The most valuable "currency" of any organization is the initiative and creativity of its members. Every leader has the solemn moral responsibility to develop these to the maximum in all his people. This is the leader's highest priority.*
>
> *W. Edwards Deming*[1]

This book won't be for everyone, especially if your stance is to sit back and watch your employees become your own personal "dance monkeys." If you're fantasizing about how to optimize your schedule to fit in your next round of golf or a pedicure, you're not a leader, and I'm not interested in helping you. Your focus, the second you signed on to this role, should have become helping the people that now report to you. If however, you are on a mission to become a better leader then, by all means, keep reading.

Some might say, "Oh, but thousands of businesses just have managers for the sake of having managers. People report to them as a formality, and that seems to be working fine!" Sure, but how many employees will stay there permanently? How many love their jobs and coworkers? How many would follow their superiors because they genuinely trust them? Corporations across the globe currently need fewer managers and more leaders. We need people who are willing to stand up for their people, no matter the cost.

Think about your organization and other organizations you interact with regularly. How many of those organizations prioritize cost-cutting as a way to survive the disruption brought on by a crisis? How many of those organizations created savings by cutting the wages and benefits of employees versus the managers, directors, and CEOs?

How many of the companies that fall in the first category are still going to be around ten years from now? And what kind of employees will

---

1. https://www.inspiringquotes.us/author/1013-w-edwards-deming

LEADERSHIP VS. MANAGEMENT

those organizations actually have? What type of relationships will these organizations have with their stakeholders and customers? Is this an organization that you would want to work for? Would you be proud when you tell people you work for them? Or would you feel a twinge of guilt because of their shady one-sided dealings that undercut the employees, but leave people who make money hand over fist nearly untouched?

In 2020, businesses were thrust into a period of disruption few could have anticipated. When the pandemic hit, societies all over the globe started asking a lot of questions about their business practices in relation to the environment. This begs the question—have corporations also entered into a period of self-reflection? Are they asking themselves the hard questions and evaluating their relationships with their employees?

We all know disruptions will happen time and time again, though how the disruption looks will differ from one instance to the next. If a business wants to survive whatever the universe can throw at them, they need strong leaders and motivated employees who are willing to fight together for the greater good of the organization.

To paraphrase John F. Kennedy now is the time for all levels of management in corporations across the globe to ask what they can do for their people, instead of what their people can do for them.

When we follow this logic from President Kennedy, I think it's high time Corporate America admits their people have not been the problem at all. The way I see it, the "elephants in the room" are the managers who have been put in charge.

Do we have people in our organizations who inspire their teams to be innovative and engaged? Do we have people in management positions who are willing to check their egos at the door? Do we have managers within organizations that align with the objectives of the organization? Or are they just looking out for their own bank accounts?

But for a moment, let's step away from the bigger philosophical questions and get back to you.

What do you hope to gain from this book?

Think about your personal motivations for a minute. Are you reading books about being a better leader, manager, or person because you assume it's expected? Or are you truly interested in becoming a better leader for the benefit of yourself, your team, and your organization?

If it's the latter, then I am truly excited and honored for the journey we are about to go on! It might be overwhelming at times, but the views from the top will be absolutely breathtaking. This process of personal growth might very well be the spark that ignites the ideas that will take you and your organization to new, unimaginable heights.

If you fall into the former category, then it is my sincere hope that you will stumble upon something on our journey that will speak to your soul. Something that will transform you from being just a manager and inspire you to become a true leader.

Brené Brown has some truly poignant thoughts on leadership, one of my favorites being that we need more leaders who commit to courageous, genuine leadership for the betterment of their people. We need leaders who have enough self-awareness to lead from their hearts. This is the kind of leader I hope to inspire you to be in the following pages as opposed to people whose guide is their ego and who use fear as a cattle prod.

Some say that leaders are born and, up to a point, I would agree. Picture your standard manager, an employee promoted to a leadership role by the higher-ups, and then picture a politician or an activist, anyone the public may choose to follow. Some people are in a leadership role because they have to be, and employees can tell their hearts aren't in it. On the other hand, some are naturally adept at slipping into leadership roles and taking charge. A few people even seem to be magnetic, the way they draw others in.

Does this mean that a person who did not show great leadership skills at the age of six will never be a good leader? Should you shy away from trying to lead your team and not just manage them if you were never in a leadership position before? Are you doomed to simply be a manager just because you were not born with a specific skill set?

The answer is a resounding NO!

I define a leader as anyone who takes responsibility for finding the potential in people[2] and processes, and who has the courage to develop that potential.

Brené Brown

If you want to go beyond being an okay manager and become an excellent leader, you can! You just have to be willing to put in the self-work. The beauty that is the human condition tells us if we set our minds on a goal, we can work to achieve it. The possibilities and potential outcomes are limitless. The question is, are you ready?

Do you need to develop your skill sets, including managerial tasks, to become an extraordinary leader?

YES!

If you want to get the absolute best out of your team, you will need to be able to lead them, not just manage them.

---

2. *https://brenebrown.com/*

Throughout this book, I will provide you with advice based on years of leadership experience, learning opportunities, time spent as a subordinate, conversations with colleagues, and research done by others related to leadership and management. I'll be giving you tools. The responsibility to develop your own unique approach to leadership to bring the best out of your people is where you come in.

The survival of any business relies on its ability to unlock the leadership qualities of its managers. These people may come from within the corporate hierarchy, from the outside, or be those individuals they wish to develop. Every person embarking on this journey needs to take the pride and ownership necessary to develop their leadership abilities. They must not only fulfill the roles and responsibilities associated with their position, but also unlock the full potential of their employees through inspirational ideas, active engagement, and encouragement to think outside the box.

During our time together, I will also provide you with some examples of men and women who excelled at being exactly what their people needed, at exactly the right time. The management and leadership skills of these people ignited positive disruptive change within themselves and others.

A significant amount of research has been done, and it pertains to both leadership and management, but don't worry; this won't be our main focus, although it can be helpful. Our main focus is becoming a great leader, which research shows as having two key terms: authentic and transformational.

A great leader is authentic; they act in real, genuine, and sincere ways that are true to who they are as individuals. They are consistent as to who they are both in and out of the work environment. More than that, a great leader is transformational. Yes, they inspire others to reach greater heights, but they also aspire to be better and develop their leadership capacity. They listen and respond to team feedback, and they grow from that feedback. (Pratt & Sales, 2018; Cherry, 2020)

This is the kind of leader I want to inspire you to be.

Chapter 1: Management vs. Leadership

Leadership and management have been used as interchangeable concepts, but in reality, they aren't. To be a leader, you will need to have qualities that extend far beyond the realm of management. Though the terms occasionally intersect, and both are aimed in the direction of a goal, the process of how you get others to reach that goal is where the key difference lies (Ward, 2020).

So, what are the key differences? And how do we go from being a manager to becoming a leader?

A manager is defined as any person who has been given the responsibility to control or direct a group of employees or a company. According to Mintzberg (Mindtools, 2009), there are 10 primary roles that a manager may be required to fulfill in the execution of their duties, and to make things simple, we'll put them into three categories:

- Interpersonal
- Informational
- Decisional

Let's break it down. *Interpersonal* describes an interaction between people; this could be between the manager and the staff, customers, or even those holding higher positions within the company. They'll need people skills to keep things moving smoothly between each group.

Informational is pretty self-explanatory, but it's harder than you may think. Managers need to provide information to each group they deal with, so they need to receive and interpret new information every day then summarize this information for their teams.

Decisional means managers will need to make decisions for their teams using whatever information is at their disposal; this can be tough, as these decisions may be challenged by future information that isn't yet known.

If all the definitions haven't made it clear yet, I'll simplify it: "manager" is a job title; "leader" is an action and a calling.

A manager is a figurehead, the top of the employee pyramid to which people report. It's merely a position of authority. However, the manager should step further and lead from that position, bringing their team to success and being the first person to step onto the battlefield despite their fears.

The job of a manager requires the monitoring of employees and mediation of both employer/employee relationships and superior/subordinate relationships. Managers represent their organization internally and, in some cases, externally. They may be responsible to share information with stakeholders and external interested parties. They ensure that whatever resources they have are distributed within the organization. This will include your workforce as well since people are the most important resource an organization will ever have.

But a leader... a leader monitors the well-being of their team. They listen to feedback and use it to grow. They know their coworkers and employees. They are trusted to help resolve interpersonal issues. Leaders communicate with their teams; even when the news is tough, they encourage and try to alleviate fear in times of uncertainty. They create positive change within the organization through problem-solving and encouraging new ideas. A leader looks out for their people, making sure that no one is left out of beneficial projects or kept from growth opportunities.

Can you tell the difference yet? There's no room for confusion. But always remember that as a leader, no matter your job title, your success is determined by the effectiveness of your team.

Some managers need to truly dedicate themselves to making the shift from manager to leader. Nayar (2014) provides the following guides against which you can measure yourself to determine if you have been successful in migrating from pure manager to true leader:

Leaders create value, while managers count value. A manager might be so focused on the specific output from an employee that they may overwhelm the person to such an extent that they can no longer add value. Let's look at an example of a floor manager at a supermarket. If they walk around from one cashier to another during the busiest time of Black Friday to find out how many people they have served, this can easily create stress and anxiety for the employees. Constantly being checked up on gives the sense of a lack of trust in the employees' capabilities. Yes, you want your company to be profitable, but employees will be more productive (and therefore create more profit) if you lead by example and enable them to be the best they can be. Instead of asking the cashiers how busy they are, step in for them to take a lunch break and man the cash register so they can be more rested for the second part of their shift.

Leaders have a sphere of influence, managers have a circle of power. Subordinates must submit to their managers, but followers choose to support a leader. If people from outside your department or reporting hierarchy come to you for advice, you are more than likely perceived as a leader by those within your work environment. Once you have cracked the code, the people within your reporting hierarchy will come to you for advice—not because they have to, but because they want to.

Leaders lead people, managers manage work. Management revolves around being able to control a group or set of entities in order to accomplish a goal. Leadership, on the other hand, speaks to a person's ability to inspire, motivate, and enable others to contribute towards the achievement of a goal. How a person influences and inspires others is often the key difference between managers and leaders. You can lead a horse to water, but you can't make it drink—a manager will try to, but a leader will provide the horse with the inspiration it needs to walk to the water and drink by itself.

This is the core of the definition of leadership—the process of inspiring others to work with you towards the achievement of a goal. Look at it this way: if you don't have others working with you towards a goal, you'll have to reach that goal alone. And chances are if you've driven your employees to that point, you deserve it. End of story.

And a final word; a chart for you to refer to in case you somehow missed everything above (Ward, 2020):

Leader	Manager
Relies heavily on interdependence	Stronger focus on top-down instructions
Inspires others to follow	Requires submission to authority
Encourages innovation	Emphasizes rationality and control
Not bound by a need to preserve the status quo	Seeks to maintain the status quo and operate within set corporate structures
Operates with relative independence	Typically, within a reporting hierarchy
Will be less focused on interpersonal issues	Will be more focused on interpersonal issues
Is a trusted guide to people around them	Is followed by necessity, not desire

It is often stated that leaders are born, not made, but I would like to argue that. Although some people may be natural-born leaders, there is not a person alive in the world that cannot learn how to lead. They just need to be given the opportunity and provided with the necessary skills to overcome the fear that is holding them back. More than that, everyone who wants to become a leader must overcome their own ego; this will separate genuine leaders from superficial ones.

If you want to excel as a boss, you cannot rely on your authority to get the job done. You will need to develop your intrinsic leadership qualities to get the best out of people. You will need to become a true leader. However, some things can seem challenging when shifting from manager to leader, such as friendships within leadership. Why? Let's dive into that for a second.

Friendship is defined as a relationship of mutual affection between people characterized by kindness, love, virtue, sympathy, honesty, altruism, loyalty, forgiveness, compassion, and trust. Within a friendship you can make mistakes without judgment, express your feelings, and be yourself—so what's the problem?

The issue develops when friendship is your only goal. If you walk in every day with your only focus to be best friends with everybody, you will be well-liked, but you may have trouble making tough decisions. Once you have crossed the line from boss to a buddy, it can become difficult to jump back to being the boss when the need arises. So should you be aloof and avoid all employee friendships? Not necessarily; if your coworkers and employees don't feel that you're a friend who looks out for them, they are less likely to turn to your leadership willingly. This presents a different problem; either way, your leadership may struggle.

The solution is to use your best judgment. While some people are adamantly against creating friendships with their employees, and sometimes even colleagues, others don't see the harm. It's all about balance and making sure no egos are bruised or in the way because, at the end of the day, we all have a job to do.

Bear Grylls stated in his 2016 book, *A Survival Guide for Life*, that your team members will start caring about what you know once they know that you care.

> *The leaders who get the most out of their people are the leaders who care the most about their people.*
>
> *Simon Sinek*

It's important to build and maintain a personal relationship with each of your team members. In this way you will slowly but surely learn more about the person behind the work masks—what hidden talents they may have, what inspires them, what motivates them, but also what may serve as a barrier to excellence.

A difficult but important thing to remember about office friendships is this; when you are in the office, everyone whether the new member or your old buddy from high school, gets treated the same. If your friend screwed up, correct them as you would any other team member and continue working.

You'll also find that being a manager is a lot like being a parent. You want what is best for your child and you will provide them with every resource and opportunity that you can afford to fulfill their potential. But you also need to set boundaries and communicate when expectations are not being met.

As an example: you know your child has the potential to go to college, so you start putting money away in a college fund. For them to go to their first-choice college, they would need to maintain a certain grade point average. Once they know the expectations for their grades, it is up to them to put in the effort to get to and maintain those grades. Let's say you then find out that your kid's grades are slipping because they have been skipping school. Most of you won't wait outside the school's exit watching to catch your son or daughter ditching class. As the loving parent that you are, you will find a way to (metaphorically) give your kid a kick in the ass instead. This way they know when a target is set and not met that there are consequences in life. And now they have to deal with those consequences and course-correct if they still hope to get into their school of choice.

Much like the scenario above, being in a role where you are required to manage the performance of your employees encompasses so much more than that. It also entails providing them with the opportunity and the resources to do their job to reasonably and effectively meet their targets. If or when targets are not met this will also include coaching and the potential reallocation of resources.

As a leader, people will need your guidance and support on a personal level as well. When they have lost their inspiration, you will need to ignite the spark deep within their soul helping them to approach their work with enthusiasm. When times get tough, they will look to you as a beacon of hope. You need to show them everything will be okay in the end. So whether you want to or not, you will need to put your big kid pants on and show the hell up when they need you. When it comes to being a leader, the team must see that you are willing to get in the trenches with them and fight whatever battle lies ahead.

Leadership is not a rank or a position, it is a choice–a choice to look after the person to the left of us and the person to the right of us.

Simon Sinek

And I couldn't agree with Mr. Simon Sinek more.

Chapter 2: What Does it Take to Be a Good Leader

When it comes to fighting in the trenches with your people, few historical leaders can be eclipsed by Mahatma Gandhi. Gandhi somehow got it right in all aspects of being a leader, in both the soul of the matter and the title (Madhusudan, 2017). Now, you might ask, what made Gandhi such a great leader? What did he achieve that was so significant? Well... that diminutive Indian man with the round glasses managed to negotiate independence for the country that's currently considered the largest democracy in the world. All without firing a single bullet.

According to Madhusudan (2017), he achieved this because of the following:

He had a rock-solid value system built around envisioning a future everybody could believe in. He enabled those around him to help achieve this goal by empowering his followers. He did this by giving them the information they needed to support the vision and energizing them to carry out what needed to be done. Interdependence was key to his ultimate success.

No matter how hard it got, he walked the talk in every way and at every level. For him, this meant to dress and live as the poorest people of his country did; the people he was fighting for.

To succeed, he had to be persistent. When things got tough, he pushed through, because he knew he was doing it for something much bigger than himself. He sacrificed his own comfort for the sake of the greater good, for what he believed in, and what he ultimately accomplished.

He was articulate. No one was standing around wondering what his purpose was or what he was working for; people knew what he stood for and why he was on this path. There was no confusion as to what he stood for, and he made sure of that.

An often-overlooked factor was that he knew how to communicate en masse. His message wasn't lost on anyone in a crowd; everyone knew what he meant. He put together and communicated plans for his vision. He played to his strengths in front of the media and his followers to explain what he wanted effectively.

He remained flexible. Although his vision never changed, when he needed to, he was able to reinvent the rules of the game to deal with the curve balls that came his way. When resources dried up, he did not beg, borrow, or steal, but instead found ways to pull together to create the resources he needed.

Read through this list again and then go back to the roles that a leader needs to fulfill. Do you see the correlation between how Gandhi approached his work and where he used his leadership skills? This is why we often admire Gandhi as a leader.

Though Gandhi was a great leader, I don't want you to become him. Learn from him, but only to gain insights on how you can transform your own managerial approach to become a leader; remain authentic to yourself. Always stay true to who you are and what you believe in your core. Then translate that into how you outwardly convey yourself in your role.

This is not a self-help book full of beautiful and powerful affirmations that will inspire some Kumbaya moment in you on a corporate retreat. But I am going to ask you to take a moment to reflect on why *you* are important. The world doesn't need another Gandhi. The world needs you to be the best version of yourself.

Yes, Gandhi was a fucking legend, but you can be one too (if you just get out of your own way).

Wherever you are along the road of your life, you are in exactly the right place to fulfill your leadership potential. The question is, are you the best version of yourself that you need to be to fulfill that purpose?

I can't help you in figuring out what your purpose is, but if you have been given an opportunity to lead a team, I *can* help you with that. Throughout our journey together, my goal is to help you learn to inspire greatness in those who will cross your path. And maybe, just maybe, even inspire others to step into a leadership role of their own.

To quote Simon Sinek again (if you don't know who he is you're missing out), "A leader's job is not to do the work for others. It's to help others figure out how to do it themselves to get things done, and to succeed beyond what they thought possible." This is the mark of a true leader. Someone who inspires and supports their people no matter the circumstance, situation, or potential outcome.

Be Authentic

A leadership role is not an audition for *The Greatest Showman—Wall Street Edition*. Your team members will not trust you or respond positively to you if you merely play the role of manager: an airbrushed, waxy embodiment of a suit and tie. The team needs you to be the real you, warts and all. Knowing that you are human will make them realize it's okay for them to be human as well. And if you're thinking it isn't–reality check, it is. It is not something to try and outrun, rather it's something to embrace. As flawed as we are, there is beauty in it because there is always an opportunity to learn and grow from our "mistakes". As I don't believe mistakes exist, only opportunities to learn, grown, and develop. Some might even call them opportunities for improvement.

When you are authentic, you are your true, genuine self. An authentic Rolex will always have more value than a knock-off and the same holds true for people. Yes—both watches can tell time, but the knock-off will never be able to compare with the craftsmanship, longevity, and authenticity of the Rolex.

With each bit of research that is done on the concept of authentic leadership, a new slant is placed on the concept, but Kruse (2013) highlights the following as common elements:

Authentic leaders are self-aware and genuine. They know their strengths and weaknesses. They do not hide their true selves, their core values and beliefs—who they are in private is exactly the same as who they are at work. They are not afraid to admit when they have made a mistake or that they don't know the answer.

Authentic leaders are mission-driven and focused on results. They put the goals of the organization ahead of their personal self-interest. Like looking good in front of their boss, or doing whatever they have to for the next shiny promotion being dangled their way.

Authentic leaders lead with their hearts. Though they still apply thinking to what they do, they are not afraid to show emotions and be vulnerable. They communicate in a very direct manner, but with empathy.

Authentic leaders focus on the long term. Long-term value creation will contribute much more to the overall sustainability of an organization than a quarterly pursuit of target beating. To nurture a company and individuals will require effort and patience, but will create much greater rewards in the end.

To make the unique approach of authentic leaders a bit clearer, let's look at how The Leadership Institute (2020) compared authentic leadership to "traditional" leadership (like the stereotypical manager who hires, fires, and leaves early to golf):

Authentic Leaders	Traditional Leaders
Lead with purpose	Lead with goals
Lead with values and principles	Can be more selfish in terms of their agenda
Lead with heart	Lead with their ego
Lead by cultivating long-term relationships	Lead by accumulating transactions
Lead by demonstrating excellence through self-discipline	Lead by imposing power and authority or leading by fear and control

Authentic leaders are most often the people who had to work a little bit harder to get where they are today. They took the responsibility of improving themselves. They realized there is a purpose to their life, so they've developed themselves to achieve that purpose.

Realizing your purpose is probably the most significant defining aspect of every person's leadership journey. This sentiment couldn't be more true for Malala Yousafzai, who will undoubtedly become one of the greatest examples of leading with purpose our world has ever seen. With a strong passion behind her beliefs, she is driven to excite change in her country, and the world at large, in ways she never expected or imagined.

Malala is the youngest Nobel Prize laureate, as of this writing, receiving this prestigious award at only 17 years old. That honor was bestowed upon her after she survived being shot by the local Pakistani Taliban in her home province because of her advocacy for female education. After waking up in a hospital 10 days later, she knew she had a choice to make. Either stay quiet, make herself small, and remain in the shadows, or use this experience as an opportunity to reach a larger audience. She chose the latter following her passion and her purpose along with this newly found platform to spread her message regarding the importance of education for girls.

For Malala, her leadership journey began when she was barely a teenager with all the odds stacked against her. She had a vision that drove her and a passion that gave her purpose, even though she had no position of power.

Now, imagine the difference you can make in your organization. Think about it. What would happen if you were able to not only find your own purpose but also create a path and ignite a purpose within your team? The added advantage you have is you don't need to survive an assassination attempt to live your purpose; you just need to find your way towards being a more authentic leader.

The Leadership Institute (2020) provides a nice five-step process for defining your path towards authentic leadership, as well as a few questions to get you on the way as well:

Step 1—Know your purpose

How do you create value for others? Why do you do what you do?

Step 2—Know your values and principles

What are your four critical values for doing good work? What actions or decisions demonstrate your values?

Step 3—Know if you have the heart for leadership

Why should people be led by you? How can you support others to be more successful?

Step 4—Know the relationships you want to cultivate

Within your team, who do you hire, fire, develop and promote? How do you choose your customers and partners? What lifetime value can you offer them?

Step 5—Know how to master self-discipline

What are your weaknesses? What are the actions that will help you overcome your weaknesses?

Now, the questions above were not included solely for your entertainment. I want you to take a pen and paper, or a spreadsheet if you are so inclined, and discover *your* answers to each. If you can't come up with an answer, think about them until you find one; dig deep. Who are you, authentically at your core? Once you've discovered who you really are at your core, check your list at least once a year. What are the lessons you have learned over the past year, and where have you

LEADERSHIP VS. MANAGEMENT

made improvements? Are you still the leader you set out to be? What has changed? What works? What doesn't? As a good leader, you should constantly be looking at yourself and exploring how, when, and where you can improve. Because there is always room for improvement and a great first step is to reach out to your employees and co-workers for honest, constructive feedback.

If you want to be an authentic leader, you should already know it will require continuous investment from you to be a little better today than you were yesterday. Who you are at your core may change over time but as long as you keep on moving forward, you are already doing better than most. And moving forward in your journey of authenticity is the first step to becoming an authentic person and an authentic leader.

Leading by Example

A major key to becoming an authentic leader is leading by example, so let's paint a little picture to help illustrate this point. Imagine there is a massive deadline approaching. Everybody is stressed, and emotions are running high. A critical element of the project just failed. In short, it's a shitshow out there. Weekend plans will need to be canceled. Everyone will need to stay late and it's already 7:10 on Friday evening, and the entire team is starving. You walk up to your manager's office to ask for permission to use the company's credit card to buy dinner for the team. You knock on their door—no answer. You ask around. Nobody has seen him since earlier in the day. You call him—sorry, he can't talk right now; he's at his daughter's dance recital. The same recital you were supposed to attend for your daughter.

What do you think just happened to the relationship between the team and their manager? Do you think the deadline is going to be reached? Goodwill and enthusiasm have officially walked out the door—and for good reason.

According to Marinuzzi (2018), the greatest killers of team morale are managers who expect others to do what they say, but not do what they do. People feel betrayed when somebody says one thing and then does another. Or when the expectations they are held to differ from that of the staff and leadership teams. Remember the dance recital?

A big determiner of the success along your journey as a leader is how well you lead others merely by example. Let's look at Gandhi again. He did not preach independence and equality from the balcony of a 5-star hotel. He lived most of his adult life in the way the majority of the people he was fighting for lived. He proved what could be possible through everything he did. He walked the walk.

When you lead by example, you create a picture of what is possible.

Read that again.

When you lead by example, you create a picture of what is possible.

And when you don't, when your expectations of the team don't match what you yourself are willing to do, more than morale will suffer.

Leading by example creates trust both within the team and between the team and their leader. As soon as you do something different from what you expect your team to do, they will stop wanting to work for you. Worse, they'll stop working hard for you, especially those who always go above and beyond. Then you'll have to rely on your job title to get them to meet their deadlines, getting the absolute bare minimum from them. Doing just enough to not get fired all while conveniently coasting along. Some may even choose to leave altogether.

On the flip side, when you lead by example and you build trust with your team they will not only follow you–they'll bust their asses without even being asked. They will genuinely know you truly want the best for them and the company. They'll rely on your leadership, guidance, and support. But maybe you're lost as to how to lead by example? If so, Marinuzzi (2018) provides the following as quick wins when establishing the pattern of walking the talk in your business:

Don't ask a member of your team or company to do something if you're not willing to do it yourself. It will go even farther with your employees when you know how to do their job. This way you can and do step in to take their place so they can take their lunch break when you're scraping by just to meet a customer deadline. You're no longer just a figurehead standing on the sidelines telling people what and how to do things (when in all actuality they are the expert at their job, not you). You're showing them you respect them and what they do. You're showing them you've got their back and are willing to do whatever it takes to support them especially in times of need and crisis.

If you implement a rule, it also applies to you, your title doesn't make you exempt. If locking your computer when you step away from your workstation is company policy, don't constantly leave your computer unlocked while you go gallivanting about the office or out to lunch. And if you do, own up to it because again, you aren't above the rules no matter what your ego is telling you.

Check your behavior. If you've realized people aren't showing up to meetings on time or aren't paying attention when they're in the meeting, you'll need to set the example of how things should be done differently going forward. Make sure you show up on time, start your meetings promptly, and set the expectation that they do the same. Don't bring your phone to a meeting or put it on silent and put it away during the meeting. Be respectful of everyone's time and attention. I know these things may seem like common sense, but I'm here to tell you, common sense is not all that common. And people will easily slide on things if and when they are given the opportunity.

Even when we do everything right ourselves and completely walk the talk, if we allow others to do what they want, it will have the same impact on team morale as our inconsistent behavior. It doesn't matter if this behavior is coming from you or someone else on the team. Why would you expect anybody to toe the line (including yourself) when one team member is allowed to do as they please? So remember, nothing will demotivate an employee or drop team morale faster than watching you tolerate an employee's bad behavior.

Leading by example ultimately comes down to consistency. This applies everywhere, not only in terms of your behavior versus the rest of the team. It applies to the behavior you allow from your team members. And no matter your level of leadership, you must be consistent in terms of your expectations for yourself and others. I've been told before I'm strict but fair. The expectation is the same for everyone, it doesn't matter who you are or your job title.

Yes, this takes a lot of self-discipline, but it's worth it. When leading by example becomes the norm some incredible benefits materialize in your team and organization. There will be higher levels of trust and respect between employees and leaders, which leads to improved employee loyalty and morale. That loyalty brings improved commitment to team goals and objectives, which increases productivity and the bottom line. And who doesn't want that for their business or company?

So how can you determine whether or not you are already walking the talk as much as you talk the talk? Ask yourself a few questions: Can you give one example of where you led through your example alone? And did your actions align with the purpose/strategic intent of the organization? If not, you've got some work to do. If so, keep up the good work!

There will be very little value added to the organization if the example you are setting does not align with the purpose and strategy of the organization. In fact, your organization should let you go if this is the case. The example you set should contribute to the overall picture and not just to what would bring glory to you and your team. If you need to cut overtime costs, make sure your team has what they need to get the job done in a timely fashion. Hold them accountable to hit targets but make sure you provide them with the tools to do so. Part of accountability is having a routine and being regimented to stick to that routine.

Routines

Before we dive into workplace routines, let's take a step back and talk about your personal morning routine. Whatever happens to you, from the moment you wake up until the moment you set foot in the office, greatly contributes to the mood you are in for the rest of the day.

There is ample evidence to indicate a well-structured morning routine can be the foundation for higher levels of productivity and an overall better mindset. A good morning routine helps you prepare for the rest of the day, which puts you in control. You can include simple stress-reducing practices such as light stretching, meditation, and healthy habits into your routine. These will keep you physically and mentally healthy; in fact, a well-rounded morning routine can help you combat forgetfulness and improve your overall fitness level.

So how can you practically set up your day for success?

To start with, try to avoid hitting the snooze button. I know that can be tough especially for those of us who aren't morning people, myself included! It's pointless to have the perfect routine on paper, or even a routine at all if you're constantly so rushed you barely have time to brush your teeth before you need to hurry out the door. The best way to avoid always wanting to hit that snooze button is by setting a reasonable wake-up time. You may also need to rethink your bedtime and nightly habits to get a good night's rest. Seems practical and easy but lack of sleep plagues our society. If this is hard to do start with small steps and then work your way up.

Secondly, avoid the early morning scroll and go for a stroll. It has become a bad habit for many of us to grab our phones the moment

LEADERSHIP VS. MANAGEMENT

we wake up mindlessly trolling the depths of the interwebs. Then we frantically realize how consumed we've been and that we no longer have time for the morning routine we'd planned. Then we're back to rushing around like a chicken with our heads cut off. So do yourself a favor and don't allow yourself to look at your phone until your morning routine is done. Instead start your day with a walk, some yoga, or stretching.

The third thing to take care of is your mind. Taking a few minutes to just find stillness within yourself—be it through prayer or meditation—puts you in a state of calm rather than stress. I also love to incorporate a gratitude practice and do some goal setting.

The last thing to include as part of your morning routine is breakfast. Fueling your body right at the beginning of the day will ensure higher energy levels and will mitigate mood changes brought about by a drop in blood sugar levels.

Just remember—you need to find what works for you. Some days you will be able to seamlessly run through your morning routine without a hitch. Other days you can only manage a cup of coffee and a shower. And that is perfectly okay! Just remember to be kind to yourself. Rome wasn't built in a day and routines aren't solidified in a day either. Just start small and work your way up. And don't be afraid to change up your routine. If you find things you love, stick with those. If there are things you try and you hate, then don't force yourself to do them. This is a practice that should be encouraging, uplifting, and motivational to get you in the right frame of mind, to put you at ease, and in a positive mindset. But remember, it's called a practice because it is ever-changing and evolving. Learn as you go and grow as you learn.

Now that you have set yourself up for success with a killer morning routine at home, you can go and do the same for yourself and your team in the workplace. But why are routines at work important? How can simple repetition be helpful at all?

As a leader when you are unpredictable both emotionally and with your expectations your employees will never know how or when to approach you. Your unpredictability could cause your employees and co-workers to avoid or even fear approaching you. Hopefully, I don't have to explain to you how bad that is for morale and business as a whole.

Your emotional responses in relation to various situations that could arise during the course of a workday will be dependent on your emotional intelligence. We'll look at emotional intelligence in depth later on. For now, let's focus on the operational component related to workplace predictability. Your routine.

Within the work environment, routines can be established in numerous ways. They can be common practice, tasks that are scheduled or even developed, and implemented into a formal process or procedure. It all depends on how in-depth and documented your organization is. I've worked in organizations with little to no documentation, just the basics. While others had everything documented into a procedure, and if there wasn't one, they would create it (which turned into a running joke with my colleagues, "There isn't a procedure? Don't worry, we'll make one!"). All of these ways will create a more stable/predictable work environment. When you have a set routine every day it removes the question of what is expected or what information is needed. This, in turn, allows for increased productivity while potentially highlighting underlying problems within the business. As long as these tasks, activities, and routines don't go overboard – you can't spend your entire day in meetings or tracking tasks because this eventually becomes cumbersome and ineffective. It's all about balance.

Now, you may start worrying about what these routines should look like, but don't panic! It doesn't have to be complicated. Vrabie (2014) provides a few simple examples of routines that can be implemented in your workplace. You can have weekly lunch meetings in the same place, or schedule a certain time of day for "quiet work", or just have your weekly or daily check-in sessions at the same time.

Routines will be especially important when teams are working remotely or if they have flexible schedules, as this will create a greater sense of belonging, routine, and normalcy (Vrabie, 2014). While I've been in overly structured environments, and I've consulted in a work-from-home environment I can't stress enough the importance of still having a routine to give you a sense of normalcy and a push to accomplish those items on your to-do list! Time blocking on your calendar to hold yourself accountable is also a super easy and effective tool for this.

But there are other advantages of having routines in the workplace, as Vrabie continues to describe. To start, there will be improved cognitive stamina, as the need for decision-making is reduced. If a team needs to make a significant number of trivial decisions throughout the day, it will result in a decrease in collaboration, communication, and innovation. By removing some of these decisions (like where to host the lunch meeting, or when everyone should check in on their goals), you're giving your employees more mental space to work on tasks, targets, and goals. You also reduce the time wasted on planning and preparation.

Routines also provide a basis for forming good habits. Repetition builds habits, and if your team struggles with collaboration, schedule a daily 10-minute session to share ideas and problems. You don't want the session to take forever and you want to schedule it at a time that isn't just convenient for you (especially last minute in a remote environment). It is incredibly frustrating when your boss doesn't take into account your schedule especially when they can't seem to be bothered. Soon you will find that collaboration will start happening naturally! This will also be a huge sigh of relief for you as a manager-turned-leader.

There will also be more consistency in the performance of certain tasks. Sometimes tasks become a little "personalized" over time; this isn't necessarily a bad thing, but most "personalization" is just laziness, which causes steps to be skipped. By creating routines for certain tasks, you can be assured that the job will be done sufficiently every time, no matter who performs it (Scivicque, 2019).

Even though I've mentioned it before, it is crucial to remember that although it is good to have some routine within the workplace, having too strict a regimen will hurt creativity. It will be important to find a balance that will work for the team, so make sure you consult them on their ideas for structure, balance, and creativity. And this may seem like a given but, don't force your ideas on them or just make the decision and move on without actually getting their input. There is nothing worse than when your boss asks for input and ideas then blindly moves forward (probably out of sheer excitement and with the best of intentions) without actually waiting for said input or considering it. This KILLS creativity and the feeling of belonging to the team. It's like the sticky part of the adhesive when left directly in the sun all day, it just melts away.

If a new routine is introduced as a formal process, it's important to monitor the change to sure the buy-in of the team. Initial resistance to change is normal and innately built into our DNA. Don't focus on this normal resistance when determining if a new process is worth keeping, but don't ignore the team's feedback either. You want to make sure that if the process overall works, you keep it. However, some tweaks here and there could be completely necessary to ensure the flow of ease within the process. Compromise is key.

Miller (2020) provides the following steps for change management as it pertains to schedules and procedures:

- Ensure that there is a definitive "why" behind the need to change. Change without purpose will just contribute to uncertainty and conflict. Make sure everyone affected by it is aware of the need for this change.

- Plan the implementation. Some changes can be introduced instantaneously while others would need to be introduced "bit by bit."

- Implement the change.

- Avoid backsliding into old habits.

- Review progress and be honest with yourself in terms of the results achieved.

The biggest factor (that should always be part of any change) is communication. If you are making decisions that will affect another team member without them being part of the conversation, you will lose the trust of the affected team member. Communication about the change is also key during the review part of the process. Your team members may have issues with the change that you aren't aware of because you never bothered to ask. Not everyone is going to speak up when they have something on their mind. So be the leader...and take the lead.

Attitude Gives Altitude

Leaders do not look for recognition from others, leaders look for others to recognize.

Simon Sinek

Hopefully, the lightbulb moment for you was long before you read this sentence. Ultimately when it comes to leadership it is about your team—not about you.

Let's look at that again, shall we?

Leadership is about *your team*. NOT about you.

Feel free to reread that last part as many times as it takes to sink in before moving on...but if you don't understand why, let me break it down for you.

If you want to parade around the building showing everybody how big your ego is, it would be best to walk straight back to your car and go home. The team is not there to make you look good. You are there to make *them* look good. Not only that, but without the team, your position is useless; that's why it's called a team. Running a business is not a one-person show. Sorry folks, but that's the reality of it.

But there is hope for those who thought they were bigshots; you can still become a good leader! It just won't happen overnight. Once you accept becoming a good leader is a process, but one that is possible, you can start down the path—you just have to have the right mindset.

Daskal (2017) provides some insight with regards to qualities that all good leaders should have and these include curiosity, positivity, empathy, communication, and resourcefulness.

Though all qualities aren't created equal, one that stands out for me the most, and offers the greatest opportunity for change comes from positivity. With a positive mindset, you can change any setback into an opportunity. If the manager brings up a problem for every solution soon the team will start to copy this behavior and a general lethargy will settle over the team. Deadlines will be missed, innovation will dry up, and problem-solving will disappear.

The reason a positive mindset spreads through a team is tied to the fact that positivity tends to breed excitement and enthusiasm. When people are excited about a new idea or challenge, they will put in more effort to make it work. Once they start engaging their "thinking" brains, more will be done to change the vision into a reality. Creativity thrives within a positive mindset.

Reh (2020) provides an example of how easy it is to flip the negativity switch through the use of words alone. Saying, "Great idea guys, but we don't have the budget for it now," might discourage the team. Saying the same thing with a positive spin can make a huge difference in how the team moves forward. So try this instead, "Great idea guys, now we have to find a way to get the funds or reallocate what we have so we can execute these ideas." You are basically saying the same thing, only one path will get you the results you desire.

As a leader, you will often be faced with situations that are beyond your control, but how you respond to those situations is 100% within your control. Only you can motivate yourself, and only you can decide whether or not you are going to face the day with a positive attitude regardless of what the day may bring. And don't forget this positive mindset starts with a great morning routine.

Since your mindset or attitude is reflected by your emotions, and your emotions guide your actions–all of which are in your control because you create the mindset you're working with. The science behind this is actually quite fascinating. Have you ever heard the phrase, "neurons that fire together wire together"? Simply put, if you look for the positive in things you will have a positive mindset, emotions, and actions. If you continue to train yourself to look for the positives it will become easier and easier over time until it is second nature–going back to those neurons. You'll create new neural pathways in your brain of positivity, hope, and optimism. So if you get your act together, those around you will follow suit. If you don't believe me, just observe your surroundings—if one person walks in the door, complaining that this Wednesday is probably the Bluest Monday they have ever faced, within an hour everybody in the office will be agreeing and complaining. Or as we used to say, "Just another day in paradise" always dripping with sarcasm and disdain as we rolled our eyes and were off to the next. Hearing a downtrodden response of agreement from our counterparts.

Emotions spread. So, try to spread positivity and encouragement where you can when you can.

As with everything, there are two sides to this coin, and you need to be careful not to spread toxic positivity. Torres (2020) defines toxic positivity as the practice of suppressing real negative emotions with positive dismissive responses. These are meant to be comforting but end up making a person feel as if their feelings and experiences don't matter.

What are a few scenarios that could potentially be found in a workplace where toxic positivity has become a bad habit? The most glaring example of this toxic positivity is when employees are told they should be positive when they have legitimate concerns instead of listening to their concerns and dealing with the issue, e.g., a female employee

LEADERSHIP VS. MANAGEMENT

raising concerns about an older, male employee's predatory behavior, and her manager telling her, "Don't worry, he is retiring in a year."

One of the most hurtful and unhealthy scenarios are those instances where employees have experienced real loss or uncertainty and colleagues tell them to look on the bright side. Such as a female colleague "comforting" another female colleague who recently had a miscarriage by telling her, "At least you don't have to worry about losing all the post-pregnancy weight."

Forced positivity will only lead to negative emotions such as depression and anxiety—so sometimes being negative can actually be positive. Calling a shit situation by its name will always yield more results than throwing platitudes such as "look on the bright side" and "it could always be worse."

You must learn how to respond to a negative situation with a positive mindset. You can learn how to admit, "Yes, this is a shitty situation, but what lesson can we learn from it or how can we fix it?"

In short, toxic positivity is choosing ignorance, which isn't bliss. It's a recipe for utter disaster. But, if you're aware and putting effort in, you can avoid it and strike a balance.

Learn to practice active listening to ensure that you can hear and validate the emotional experiences of those around you. Encourage honest problem identification. Allow them to experience negative emotions, but also provide space for finding solutions to those concerns. Be honest, and face your hardships and difficulties, though be careful not to discourage your team. To do this, you must develop empathy and ensure that your team feels safe physically and psychologically.

At the end of the day, you need to create an environment in which your team feels heard and encouraged, so you can tackle the problems you may face head-on. Your team will mimic your mindset—don't put anything out there you are not willing to deal with when radiated back at you. And remember the best gift to give your team is not a coffee machine—it is the best version of yourself.

If your actions inspire others to dream more, learn more and do more, you are a leader.

John Quincy Jones

Working Towards a Goal

According to Gallo (2011), one of the most critical components of any manager's job will be to support employees in the process of setting and reaching goals. People want to see how their work feeds into larger objectives. If the right goals are set for them, and they can see the connection between what they do and how their goals contribute, intrinsic motivation and efficiency will increase greatly.

Motivation–nonsense. All that people need to know is why their work is important.

W. Edwards Deming

Although there is a fine line between helping an employee set up their own goals and setting goals for them. If an employee feels they have no say or power in their goals, they will take minimal ownership of the goal and will be less motivated to achieve it. They will do it because they have to, not because they want to. But if you help them discover their personal goals, they'll own them because they weren't badgered into picking a generic goal by a manager breathing down their necks.

Gallo (2011) lists the following principles for supporting your team in reaching their objectives:

Connect personal goals towards organizational goals. The first step would be to make sure employees understand the organization's goals. You will be fighting a losing battle if you try to link their goals to the bigger company goals if they don't know the company-specific goals. Once you are sure they understand where the organization is headed, help them to align their goals with company goals but also understand how they align. Helping them to see the bigger picture will make them feel more inclusive when it comes to what the company is doing. And if they have no idea what goals they want to set, this may also help them to drum up some ideas. So let them know what the company's goals are and give them some time to create goals on their own first, so it doesn't feel like these goals are being forced on them.

Make sure goals will challenge the team while remaining achievable. Allow an employee to set up a list of goals they want to achieve and link them to the overall goals of the organization. This should be easy to do since you've already discussed what the company goals are and coached them through aligning their goals to that of the company. Once this is done, it is your duty as their leader to have a discussion with your employee to ensure their targets are realistic, while still challenging them. Making sure employees are challenged through their goals, but not overwhelmed by the magnitude can easily be the difference between growth and giving up.

Create a plan for success. A goal means nothing if it is not backed up by a plan. This effectively means breaking the goal down into small tasks with due dates attached. Tasks and due dates should also be agreed upon, not just doled out. Just because you could have the task completed in a week doesn't mean they will. Not everyone is you or has your level of expertise so get their buy-in first. This may mean setting aside time to meet with them to discuss and decide upon tasks and deadlines together. When they have more say in task setting and deadlines, they'll also take more ownership to complete targets on time.

It's also always a good idea to make sure they understand what they will need from others in order to achieve their goal and what they need to do in order to get the support they require. If they don't understand or know where to look for help that's where you come in. Some of your team will take off like rockets and others will require a little more help. As long as they know you support them and you've got their back, they

LEADERSHIP VS. MANAGEMENT 41

should willingly come to you if a deadline can't be met or a roadblock pops up. Make sure they know you're here to help and in their corner. Tell them if roadblocks arise or timing is threatened to always come to you for support. After all, you are a team and that is your job as the manager and this is a crucial difference between leading (being supportive) and managing (taskmaster).

Monitor progress. It's one thing to monitor someone's progress as their boss but another thing entirely to actively engage them in monitoring their goals together. You can do this through conversations about their goals, upcoming deadlines, and see what resources or additional support they need to achieve these goals based on their current progress. Think of it as a pulse check on where they are at – by you taking the time to check in they know you are there to support them and it helps to keep the task deadlines in the forefront of everyone's mind. As their leader, it is your duty to break down any barriers and roadblocks that may be standing in the way of your employees reaching their goals. The best way to do this is to check in with the team weekly, or some predetermined increment of time.

When you're checking in consistently any issues can be resolved quickly. Then your team will have an incentive to be further along in their progress toward their goals at the next check-in. Monitoring goals with them also gives you both an opportunity to stay on track toward meeting goals. This way sudden speed bumps or huge roadblocks make themselves known sooner and won't be ignored. It's incredibly easy for time to get away from you and to not be able to make up lost ground if you aren't checking in on a regular basis. You also may need to adjust the schedule pending the progress that is being made.

Respond to storms that may arise. Building on the previous point, employees should be comfortable coming to you when things go wrong or if it looks as if things might not pan out according to plan. When problems do arise, don't try to be the hero and fix the problem. Allow the employee to first seek their own solutions and only coach and advise them.

In some cases, you even have to take a step back and coach only when they ask for it. This is something I had to learn firsthand when one of the best supervisors took over my line after I got promoted to manager. It wasn't that trusting him was hard because he's a rockstar of a human being and kicked ass at his job. It was my ability, or in this case, inability to let go and back off that was the problem.

So you know what I did? Admitted to overstepping, apologized, told him I knew he could handle it, and told him to call me out when I did it again. He immediately heckled me telling me, "You do that *a lot*!" We laughed about it, moved on, and he called me out on it from then on whenever I did it. Which eventually became few and far between because we had that open line of communication. This is also how you build trust with your team. He knew I had his back and I knew he had mine. But if an issue still persists, step in, but not before the employee has tried to resolve it themselves. Give them their chance, you might even be pleasantly surprised by the outcome.

On a more personal level, if you can help an employee see the link between their personal purpose in life and how they contribute to the organization, you will be able to provide even greater opportunities for the employee to contribute.

Let's make this a bit more practical. Say you have an employee, let's call her Sara, who is always volunteering with various charities. You obviously have somebody who has a drive and feels a sense of purpose to help others. Sara is also the administrative assistant for the team. Lately, there have been a few delays at work because stationary and other smaller tools and equipment are not being ordered on time. Other team members are planning a revolt, as they feel Sara is

LEADERSHIP VS. MANAGEMENT

constantly busy on the phone planning the next charity event instead of doing what she needs to do at the office.

Now, as a manager you have three options: (A) let the other employees deal with Sara, that way your hands remain clean, (B) have a hard performance discussion with Sara and give her a warning, or (C) have a conversation about goals and purpose.

The default setting for most managers will result in option two being taken, and I'm no exception to this rule. But we want to be effective leaders, not managers. So for the fun of it, let's quickly discuss the merits of option three.

You know Sara loves helping people. What if you help her see that by supporting the rest of the team with what they need more effectively and efficiently, Sara would in fact be helping people. It might be considered "common sense" for the administrative assistant to support the team. But by helping her see the link between her personal purpose and how she performs her job on a daily basis, her internal motivations to do and be better will be much stronger. Bonus for you, she'll be doing her job better and feel personal fulfillment.

Everyone tends to perform better and work harder to achieve a goal if the source of motivation is internal, rather than external. To clarify, I do NOT mean the motivation that makes you ready and willing to clean your house when you feel like it; the motivation I'm referring to is the internal drive that gains satisfaction by certain tasks. As an example, I don't always *feel* like cooking for my family, but the satisfaction I receive when everyone is happy and full drives me to do it again and again. That's the motivation I'm talking about, the driving force for my actions.

In order to empower your employees to ignite their own internal sources of motivation, you will need to have conversations with them to understand what gives them joy and direction in life. These conversations should be natural and heart-felt since people won't easily share their aspirations if they feel you're being insincere. Make sure you take the time to have an honest uninterrupted conversation.

Getting back to Sara: her motivation is to help people, so she chooses tasks that help people. By reminding Sara how her job helps people and allowing her to take ownership of her path, you will alleviate the concerns raised by the team. Also ensuring greater commitment to the tasks at hand.

Although, sometimes (despite your best intentions) shit will still hit the fan, and goals will not be met—what then? Participation awards in business are not a cornerstone of success. So a pat on the back and an, "Oh well, at least you tried," will be the end of you, your team, and the organization if that is your go-to approach whenever a target is not met.

But you don't have to go in guns blazing and fire everybody to hold people accountable when a goal is not met either. Going from one extreme to the other won't solve any of your problems. It will actually create more. You just need to understand why things went wrong and what needs to be done to prevent failure again in the future. Instead, put a positive spin on things and take it as an opportunity to learn, or a growth opportunity. Failure is just as much about learning as it is an opportunity to make that positive shift in your mindset.

Some people may give up at this point, saying that it's too hard to set personal goals for themselves and others. Is it even worth it?

LEADERSHIP VS. MANAGEMENT

Yes, it can be hard. And yes, it's worth it. Employees who seek to fulfill personal goals at your company will be more inclined to stay and grow with you, while actually enjoying their work. And goal setting doesn't have to be complicated. Per Gallo (2011), here are some general principles to remember when it comes to setting goals:

Do	Don't
Connect individual goals to bigger objectives within the organization.	Expect employees to set goals alone.
Ensure that your team understands you are a partner in achieving their goals.	Take a hand's off approach to high performers. (Even though they do well on their own, they will still benefit from your input and feedback.)
Connect personal purpose and interests to professional goals.	Ignore failures.

Whenever you see a successful business, someone once made a courageous decision.

Peter F. Drucker

Decision Making

When it comes to decision making one of the most frustrating things I've seen is when managers cannot make a decision. Sometimes I can't help but think, "You're supposed to be the experts, the people calling the shots so why the hell are we paying you a big salary if you don't have the balls to make a decision?" The same is true when it comes to you and your people.

Your subordinates need you to make clear and consistent decisions on a daily basis—not just your superiors. Whatever you decide, commit to it and communicate the decision to those who might be affected by it. You also want to include anyone who would need to support you in the execution of tasks related to it. Remember: there's no "I" in "team."

When you need to make the final decision, call on your team to provide you with their insights. In most cases, they may challenge the view you originally had and allow you to see aspects you may have overlooked. Since they are the ones dealing with the process, materials, people, and equipment on a daily basis they ARE your experts. Never forget that. I don't care how many degrees you have or how long you've "been doing this." This is a particular phrase I've come to loathe from arrogant short-sided managers over the years. Statements like this come from someone stuck in a managerial hierarchy operating solely from their ego with a slim hope of ever truly becoming a leader. We must remember our people, for they are always our best source of information because their knowledge is irreplaceable. A manager who thinks they always know everything and know better than their people is really someone who isn't willing to listen or take advice from others. Collaboration is the secret to success. Never forget that.

Anytime you're facing complex, high-pressure circumstances, deadlines, and confusing information, remember this is just the reality of being a leader. And through all of this, it is still your responsibility to take whatever ambiguity that you and your team may be facing and create clarity from it.

It's not always easy or fun to make decisions, but somebody has to do it and that's why they put you in charge! Let it be you rather than somebody else making decisions on behalf of your department. There is nothing more frustrating than someone else outside of your team trying to make decisions on something they know little to nothing about. You know the ins and outs of your team and your business. This is why you and your people are the best suited for this job! One of the best ways for a manager to show they can be a leader is through decision-making. It's one of the ways you can be a guiding light when the fog of pressure starts setting in. So be strong and stand tall; you've got this. And lean on your people for support.

Winterhalter (2020) lists the following as the five critical decision-making skills that every manager should develop:

- Identify critical factors that will affect the outcome of a decision. Analytical and interpretive skills are required for this, as you will use them to figure out everything that needs to be considered during the decision-making and implementation stage.

- Evaluate options and establish priorities accurately. With every decision, there are at least two paths to take, and being able to assess the quality of the alternatives is essential.

- Anticipate outcomes and see logical consequences. This is also generally referred to as scenario planning. It's part of the overall risk management process involved in decision-making. You will need to be able to determine what the consequences of each decision could be to the best of your ability.

- Navigate risk and uncertainty. With every decision, there will be uncertainty, regardless of how much you have tried to evaluate every possible outcome. At the end of the day, you have to go with your gut and stick to your guns. If you believe in yourself, your process, and above all else, your people, the rest will work itself out.

- Analyzing, interpreting, and evaluating vital information is a requirement in the decision-making process to ensure that you can respond effectively to the unknowns that may pop up along the way.

In the end, your ability to make decisions will be affected by the cohesiveness of your team. If you are effectively leading your team, they will provide you with information and insights that could significantly improve your ability to make a decision. They cannot make the decision on your behalf, but if the team is disjointed and unmotivated, you will not be getting the information or support that may be required.

The fear of making the wrong decision is what often keeps people from making a decision. This indecision can be more deadly to a business than the wrong decision.

Your team will only be as strong as the decisions you make. The wrong decision is still better than no decision because at least you have picked a direction to go. Let's look at a hypothetical scenario to illustrate the point.

Imagine you are walking on a physical path; sometimes there may be rocks and boulders in the way. Occasionally, there are small streams or poison ivy to navigate, and there may even be predators that try to attack you. Now, every decision you make will happen at a crossroads on this journey. Sometimes it might just be a little gravel sidetrack that will eventually take you back to the original path. Under other circumstances, it may be a completely new direction that you, your team, and the organization will head in. Sometimes you will be able to see miles in front of you. At other times, you will be covered in a blanket of darkness and will barely be able to shuffle ahead one step at a time.

Regardless of how the road ahead looks, you always need to keep moving because you are not the only one on this road. If you get stuck on making a decision for too long, others will pass you by and certain opportunities might be lost forever. But if you make the decision too quickly, you might end up in a swampy marsh. So yes, there is a delicate balance to maintain when it comes to the speed at which decisions should be made, and this will vary from one situation to another. Sometimes you will get it wrong, but it's better to deal with the consequences of a wrong decision rather than the consequences of no decision at all. Remember every choice we make in life is another opportunity to learn.

Chapter 3: What Good Leaders Look For

A company could put a top man at every position and be swallowed by a competitor with people only half as good, but who are working together.

W. Edwards Deming

Only a few lucky team leaders will have the opportunity to build their team from the ground up. It is far more likely you will have inherited the team that you are now expected to lead.

Whether or not you get to choose the people on your team or if you've been chosen to lead an existing team, the responsibilities are still the same. It will be up to you to align your people and help them to achieve optimal performance toward the organizational goals. If you fail at that, you have failed at being both a manager and a leader.

Defining Teams and Teamwork

A team can be defined as a group of people organized together to perform tasks in pursuit of a common goal. Teams are often put together when the scope of work to be performed is too big for just one person to handle. Each member of the team is chosen based on their unique set of skills, but if they can't work as part of the team, their overall contribution to the greater good will be lost.

Teamwork, as I'm sure you're aware, involves individuals performing interdependent activities in the pursuit of set goals. In order for a team to function effectively, it will need to have shared values, trust, inspirational leadership, skilled members, and good communication.

It is important to understand that conflict will be inevitable. A team without conflict is often a team that is actually not working together, or even attempting to work together.

One of the reasons why teams can contribute so much success to an organization is because of the diversity in views, skills, and attributes that are accumulated when individuals are combined into a unit. Diversity is vital to the survival of a team. Without it, the team may experience "groupthink," which occurs when people are so focused on being liked that no one actually contributes original thought. However, diversity can also potentially cause conflict. But, if used effectively, conflict can result in innovation. If not managed properly, it will result in complete dysfunction.

Dealing with Dysfunctional Teams

Whenever there is a personnel change within a team, or a dynamic change in how the team operates (office-bound vs. remote), the team will need to recenter and adapt to the new changes. Team development happens according to natural patterns, and you will need to be able to identify which stage of development your team is in and how to support them through the process.

Scully (2020) provides the following summary of Bruce Wayne Tuckman's team development model:

Forming: This happens during the initial establishment of the team; details are given regarding expectations and responsibilities are assigned.

Storming: Ideas are shared. Some team members may use this as an opportunity to either improve their standing in the pecking order or to facilitate acceptance by the team. Competition may emerge within the team, and communication can become strained.

Norming: The team has now entered "calm seas" and everybody is working well together. Efficiency is nearly optimized, as everybody is communicating well and working toward the same goal.

Performing: Trust is at optimal levels and individuals are operating at peak efficiency with less oversight from leaders. There may still be issues, but team members are able to solve their own problems with limited inputs from the manager required.

LEADERSHIP VS. MANAGEMENT

Adjourning: This phase is entered into when a team that was set up for a specific project only, or when a big project within a normal functional unit has been completed.

When your team is in the throes of the storming process, it may very well resemble a dysfunctional team, but dysfunction can happen at any level of the process. Though it is normal for things to not always run smoothly within a team, you will need to be able to identify when serious interventions are required.

Luckily, there are some signs to look out for that indicate a team heading to dysfunction. Forbes Coaches Council (2016) says to watch for a breakdown in communication, absence of trust, unresolved conflicts, and mass exodus of talent. You may also see team members becoming withdrawn, or overly comfortable to the point of tattling, avoiding decision-making, or blame-shifting. When you see employees "operating in silos," which means working without communicating any information or interacting with others, you have a problem. And if you also see formations of subgroups within your team where members are fixated on only the problems, both past and current, then you're in the "danger zone," my friend.

How these dysfunctions manifest within a team at any given period of time will be dependent on the players and the circumstances. Regardless of how they look or why they occurred, the sooner you act when you see the problem, the less 'rot' will spread throughout the team and organization. More often than not, you will need to address people issues instead of operational issues in order to get back on course again.

In order to address team dysfunction, there are a few steps to take. First, you need to set clear goals (which we covered previously), and a reasonable strategy to reach those goals. Make sure everyone knows what their part is, and make sure they know what the team priorities are. If you start a project with these in mind, you are set up to succeed!

On a relational level, you can address dysfunction issues by giving and receiving trust, sharing and celebrating success, and taking care of conflicts. You need to use those conflicts as opportunities for improvement and learn to value the differences within your team. This will create an atmosphere of respect and genuine appreciation that will help solve and prevent major dysfunction.

I can provide you with a very long list of why dysfunction happens in a team, but if I do that, you might be tempted to use it as a checklist to find the problem instead of actually listening and having a few hard conversations.

Leaders must either invest a reasonable amount of time attending to fears and feelings or squander an unreasonable amount of time trying to manage ineffective and unproductive behavior.

Brené Brown

Attributes of a Team Player

―――

Hire people inspired to achieve something big over people who demand something big to be inspired.

Simon Sinek

When adding someone to your team, it can be difficult to know who will both add value and grow well in the environment. I've found that Riggio (2013) summarizes the qualities that can help you evaluate whether a person would be good for your team or not.

They say a team player is honest and straightforward—they don't play games or lead others on, and they will tell you what is happening regardless of whether or not it is good news. A team player is willing to share the workload without complaining and is reliable. The person you should add is fair, and won't take credit for somebody else's work. Moreover, they complement the skills your team already has—they bring something different to the team, and are willing to share their skills and weaknesses to the benefit of the entire group.

You should NOT add someone if they don't have good communication skills, or if they have a pessimistic attitude. That negativity is contagious, and if one person in the team is constantly pessimistic, it will soon spread to the rest.

You will need to identify the characteristics your team needs in order to be able to reach the goals you have set for the team. You will also need to identify the characteristics in team members that might hamper the initial stages of team development and prevent the team from going forward toward the norming phase. In 2019, Valdez laid out some of the biggest warning signs to look out for:

Their mindset is set on maintaining the status quo. Someone who has a fixed mindset will become stuck in the need to prove themselves over and over again. They believe their qualities are carved in stone, and how things are is as good as they will get, for both themselves and the organization. These people do not try to improve or grow as a person and will not put effort into improving or growing as an organization.

Strike. One.

They are not coachable. Unfortunately, some people don't want to learn anything new, which often expands until they are unwilling to take ownership or responsibility. These people avoid introspection and emotional growth. They are focused on short-term thinking and are unwilling to try new things. They always believe they are right. I'm sure that you can imagine how this could be a problem, you may even know people like this. If a person isn't adaptable and humble, then as things change, that person will refuse to change with the team and will become obsolete.

Strike two.

They are unwilling to take direction or instruction from you. People who question every decision you make, and do what they want to do even though you request they focus on something else, will not benefit your team. They have no trust in you or your leadership, and will likely never try to build that trust. There's a difference between people sharing opposing ideas and trying to cause trouble. This characteristic only causes trouble; strike three. They're out.

If you tolerate these bad behaviors, they will become the norm. If employees are not willing to commit to the values and goals, you will need to have a conversation with them in order to understand why they are resisting. If they are unwilling to participate in the process to address their behavior or to share their concerns, it might be time to make a hard decision about the individual's future in the group. It is easier and better for the organization overall if you cut ties early on rather than continue an uphill losing battle.

A person who is not happy within their work environment will make other people unhappy as well. The entire team deserves the opportunity to work in an environment that is conducive to their mental, emotional, and physical health.

Why Teams Fail

If you want people to make the same decisions that you would make, but in a more scalable way, you have to give them the same information you have.

Keith Rabois

Despite your best efforts, your team may still occasionally fail. But before you start blaming the individual team members, look at yourself first and see whether or not there are areas of improvement within yourself. Everything starts with you and ends with you. You, as the leader, need to take responsibility and address the failure by admitting and finding the root cause of the issues. Then, you need to work with your team and address the problem. After that comes your challenge of putting the solution in place and leading your team forward.

Some failures are caused by people rather than faulty routines or equipment. Underlying fear can be one of the unspoken reasons why team members act out and cause disruptions within a team. Sometimes the fear is deeply rooted within a person's subconscious, and they themselves might not even know why they are acting the way they are, but they may be powerless to stop themselves.

You can't change them, but you can provide them with the opportunities to change themselves. They will need to go through their own growth processes, as you have, to become their most authentic selves.

In order to ensure that your team remains on the path to success, Deering (n.d) provides a list of the following habits which should be practiced in order to replace the bad habits within a team:

- Open, honest, and effective communication
- Dedicated focus on goals and results
- Everybody contributing their fair share
- Team members supporting one another
- Diverse views are shared and tolerated
- Effective leadership
- Organized tasks
- Opportunities to have fun

These points have been discussed before and will be discussed again, but it is important to remember these basics and go back to them whenever things go a bit askew in real life.

Chapter 4: Training and Empowerment

Learning is not compulsory... neither is survival.

W. Edwards Deming

Perfection does not exist. It will be damaging to your well-being, as well as your teams to try and achieve it. However, you should aim to be a bit better today than you were yesterday. Be honest with yourself about the skills you have and the skills you need to improve on.

As humans, we tend to want to stay in our comfort zones, and at work, this means we will pay the most attention to the tasks we are good at. Whether it is the fear of failure or the need to succeed that drives us to do this, is irrelevant. As long as we are only focusing on our strengths, we are not fulfilling our true purpose and potential to develop ourselves completely.

Let's look at a practical example. The five basic skills a tennis player should have to compete at any level would be backhand, forehand, serve, endurance, and agility. If the player has a naturally good forehand and weak backhand and they decide to only focus on improving their forehand, their opponents would soon realize this. Now, they just need to find a way to force them onto their backhand to put them under pressure. Regardless of how much work the player puts into all the other attributes required, as long as they neglect to work on their backhand, they will have a weakness their opponents will be able to expose and exploit. Every. Single. Time.

This holds true in any realm of your life or career, especially leadership skills. We all have attributes that come naturally to us and we would prefer to focus on them because it's easy. But unless you strengthen the weaker links in your armor, you will always have vulnerabilities.

Those vulnerabilities may not necessarily be exploited by your "competitors" within your work environment or your subordinates (unless you find yourself in a very toxic work environment), but they can very well be exploited by your own internal dialogue. We can very easily become our own worst enemy when our internal dialogue perpetuates our self-doubt by keeping us focused on our weaknesses and failures.

Your own mind and self-talk can be your biggest weakness, and in many people, it's actually one of the skills you need to develop the most. Finding the underlying source of your self-doubt is a journey in itself. One which lies far outside the realm of what we are trying to achieve in this book. Although it's worth exploring the what's and why's behind the hurdles you are dragging onto your path. But keep in mind, just as you have many skills and positive traits, you also have weaknesses to strengthen and develop.

Improving Your Own Skill Set

You will need to be brutally honest with yourself when it comes to your own weaknesses. After all, the easiest person to lie to is ourselves. If you still think you are the best thing since sliced bread, then you might need a reality check. Mindtools (2009) is very helpful in highlighting several areas in which a leader may find themselves deficient; use them to help you grow, not to discourage yourself from trying.

We'll start slowly: a good leader needs to be a good spokesperson. Public speaking will be a core skill to acquire. Communication skills, in general, are vital to leadership. Bargaining and negotiation are key elements, and these skills require practice. You may want to do research on some negotiation or bargaining techniques if this is an area you're less comfortable with.

A large portion of your communication will be non-verbal (we're taking body language here) as well as written. It would be a great idea to ask a trusted co-worker or even your boss to assess your current non-verbal communication skills. Such as, do you roll your eyes without knowing it? Do you tend to take on a defensive stance while having conversations with people, both the ones you do and do not get along with? Do you easily and quickly brush people off as if you're too busy to be bothered by them? Or do you practice active listening skills without being distracted by your surroundings or your cell phone? We've all been guilty of each of these at some point but our awareness of the issue is the first step in resolving it.

As for written communication, you can practice some of the very same things. Ask people close to you how your emails come across. Are you direct and to the point while still maintaining professionalism? Or did you write an email while you were pissed off and hit send before giving it a once over upon replying? You never want to send an email or any type of response out of anger. Paper trails, which in this modern age include chats, texts, social media posts, and voice messages, last forever and can be severely damaging to your career, if not career-ending. Even verbal communication where you think you're just blowing off steam to a colleague about someone else you work with can be detrimental and get back to them. So think before you speak and respond. You may also want to practice writing reports, or giving presentations to sprucc up your communication skills. Additionally, if you are not up to speed with the jargon used in your field, you might need to find a crash course in order to be able to facilitate effective communication. And don't be afraid to ask for help.

As for roles you need to fill, there are many. As a leader, you're a figurehead, a liaison, a mediator, and a resource allocator. In all of these, you need to look out for the best interests of your people and your company.

You may feel overwhelmed right now, and that's ok; it's understandable. But don't worry. You'll grow into your role, as long as you earnestly put effort into yourself and your people. You can read leadership books, like this one, or take classes for the other skills. See what your company has to offer, you may be surprised at the resources available to you. But here's a trade secret: all of these things will fall into place if you strengthen your emotional intelligence.

It can be easier to develop "hard" skills like budgeting or mastering a new computer program than it is to develop a "soft" skill. It is easier to know when you've grasped the basics of budgeting and other skills that have a definitive outcome. But soft skills are even more important.

One of the core soft skills any manager or leader should develop is emotional intelligence. Emotional intelligence is broadly defined as a person's capacity to be aware of their own emotions as well as knowing how to control and express them. High levels of emotional intelligence allow you to handle relationships with others more judiciously and emphatically.

Before you can do anything else, you will need to be able to perceive emotions accurately. This also involves being able to read nonverbal signals such as body language and facial expressions. Once you can perceive emotions, you can start reasoning with them. When we reason with our emotions, it doesn't mean we try to convince them to be a different type of emotion. What it does mean is we use our emotions to promote thinking helping us prioritize what we pay attention to.

The third piece of the puzzle relates to understanding the meaning attached to the emotion—is somebody angry because of something we did, or because of a different event we are not aware of? Unless you're a mind reader, which sounds horribly invasive, you won't always know unless you ask. And it's always better to ask than assume...I think we all know how that old saying goes.

Lastly, at the highest level of emotional intelligence, people are able to regulate their own emotions and respond accordingly to the emotions of others. Higher levels of emotional intelligence require greater conscious involvement, while lower levels tend to happen on a subconscious level (Cherry, 2020). In other words—all people will intrinsically be able to pick up on emotions and use them to prioritize their reactions, but not everybody will have the necessary skills to understand and regulate emotions.

This all might seem like a bunch of touchy-feely mumbo-jumbo that has no relevance when it comes to being a good leader, but Cherry

(2020) provides a few examples of how high emotional intelligence can play a role in improving our lives on a daily basis.

A person with high emotional intelligence has a greater capacity for accepting criticism and responsibility, which makes it easier to move on after mistakes. They are better at saying "no" when they need to, at sharing and understanding feelings and concerns, and therefore better at finding solutions that work for everyone. They are better listeners, less judgmental, and have a better understanding of what makes people tick. This builds trust and helps them enhance the office morale and output.

You will find once you have committed yourself to improve the attributes in relation to some of your key roles, you might already start performing better as a leader as well. When it comes to improving your leadership, there are hard and soft skills that can be learned through formal training. But there are also subtle nuances related to how the business operates outside the formal guidelines that can only be learned when you are down in the trenches with the team.

By spending time with your team, you not only get to know your team better, but you also gain insights into the experience of those whom you have the responsibility to lead. You learn who is best able to provide you with critical information; you may gain a better understanding of the challenges they face daily, but you also learn why processes are executed in a certain manner.

The purpose of learning from others is not so you can take over and do their job on their behalf. Rather it's to get a better understanding of what they experience on a daily basis and develop more empathy for them. When you understand how they do what they do by working alongside them, it builds a bond and trust that can't easily be shaken.

LEADERSHIP VS. MANAGEMENT

If you are determined to stay in your own little bubble within the work environment and continue to perpetuate this idea of "us versus them," you will continue to see the world the way you do right now. You might think there is nothing wrong with that, but you are moving into extremely dangerous territory if you cannot see this fundamental character flaw with your narrow vision.

Learning from your team improves your relationships, which increases support when you're hit with roadblocks. You also gain different perspectives and information you may not have known, which can help you overcome those hardships (Melnyck, 2019). It is also important to keep in mind that if you are new to a team or a company, your best source of information will be the people that predate you.

The goal is not to be perfect at the end, the goal is to be better today.

Simon Sinek

Improving Your Team So They Can Replace You

To build a strong team, you must see someone else's strength as a complement to your weakness, not a threat to your position or authority.

Christine Caine

I have encountered many managers who were so afraid to be outshined by their subordinates they deliberately attempted to sabotage them by withholding growth and training opportunities. Others simply didn't have the faith in their people to develop and grow into what they wanted, prejudging before ever giving them a chance to prove themselves. This leads to poor performance of the team, which leads to changes in management, or caused incredibly talented people to walk away from their boss and in some cases the company as a whole.

It all starts and ends with the leader, and in some cases, a coach.

At the time of this writing, Gregg Papovich is the head coach of the NBA team the San Antonio Spurs, according to Google, he earns around $11 million annually. Mr. Papovich has been the head coach of the Spurs since 1996. During his tenure, the team has won 67.5% of all games played and has brought home five NBA titles. The Spurs had never won an NBA title until Papovich took over as head coach of the team. What makes his tenure even more impressive is the fact that he is currently the longest-serving head coach in the NBA and all other sports leagues in the United States.

Okay, so now that you have recovered from the shock of how much money being a basketball coach earns you, we can get back to the point that I'm trying to make. Papovich has not been at the helm for so long because of his own wickedly accurate 3-pointers or any other athletic abilities that might set him apart from his coaching rivals. His success is based on the fact that he is able to identify the key strengths in each of his players and use them to the benefit of the entire team. He is also able to identify the weaknesses within his players to allow them an opportunity to improve and remain competitive on the court.

If his star player is having the game of their life, he's not going to pull them from the game because he's jealous of all the praise and attention they'll get. He knows the better his players perform, the better it will reflect on him. His success will not be measured by how awesome he himself is, but rather by how successful he can make the team and players under his tutelage.

So, how does this relate back to the boardroom?

A leader is a coach, not a judge.

W. Edwards Deming

According to Bartlett (2018), the main purpose of a coach is to improve the performance of the team. That performance is affected by many factors the coach needs to help improve. A few of those factors are the mindset of your team, the overall game plan, the team culture and environment, and interpersonal relationships.

In other words, managers and leaders are like coaches as they are responsible for maintaining and improving the performance of their teams. Just like with sports coaches, this is done through performance analysis, skills development, and emotional support.

Improving the skills of your team is just as important for you as it is for Papovich to improve the percentage of his free-throw shooters. Skill improvement happens through training. Just as it is necessary for you to grow yourself, it's also necessary to grow your team.

You must provide your team with adequate opportunities to grow and develop, even if this means they will at some point be better skilled than you. Even if this leads to their leaving your team to take a position that is better suited for their hopes and dreams. That's one of two common reasons managers do not want to allow their subordinates to improve their skills. They're afraid of employees being able to replace them and afraid of employees leaving them and taking all that knowledge (the company has paid for) with them.

It is my wholehearted belief that anything less for your people is doing them a grave disservice and is nothing less than a failure on your part. Our job as leaders is to grow and develop our people, in whatever way suits them best. We have to learn to remove ourselves from this equation because we don't matter here. It's when we let our ego step in the way that we keep people from their full potential.

Regardless of the cost and time involved with training, it is one of the things that should never be excluded from the budget. Quite frankly from a people perspective it is THE most important investment you will ever make. It improves employee performance, satisfaction, morale, and the overall workplace environment. It strengthens weaknesses by improving their knowledge and improves consistency in how tasks are performed. This, in turn, reduces resources wasted and the need for supervision. Not to mention employee turn-over at all levels of the organization. In the big picture, it increases the opportunity to promote from within, which will keep your employees around long-term. And that's what we want right? To reduce turnover and improve the amazing people we already have just waiting at our fingertips to get their chance, to become better, and to be better.

Offering those opportunities is a must but you'll have great buy-in when employees are encouraged and supported to identify their own training needs and growth opportunities. Create an understanding

LEADERSHIP VS. MANAGEMENT

with your team to be open to continuous learning, since it will hold benefits for them on a personal level. Just be sure to prepare them for increased levels of responsibility as they grow.

In tough economic times, you will need to find smart ways to continue training employees in order to avoid stagnation of skills and innovation. If employees are exposed to new information, they will take that information back to their own work and try to find ways to do what they do better. Two smart, less expensive ways of training your employees can be through on-the-job training and mentoring.

When it comes to training, a lot of new managers make the mistake of taking employees through "training" that actually serves no purpose. For example, a new hire may be taught to leave their phone in their locker and go to the manager for any purchases above five thousand dollars. When that employee moves out of training, they see everyone has their phones on them and they are rudely dismissed when contacting the manager for large purchases. In this example, the time and training were wasted because the processes aren't respected. So before you start approving training, think about the following in order to ensure whatever training your employees embark on, adds value to them and the organization:

- What does the business need?

- Will training be the right solution to address issues identified during the business needs analysis?

- What is the expected outcome of the training?

If at any stage an employee requests training that cannot be approved (like asking for tuition assistance in a job-oriented degree, but your company can't afford it) make sure you provide them with feedback as to why they cannot attend a specific training they've requested. For whatever reason. Additionally, creating some type of alternate plan to get them the training they want or something supplemental shows them you care about them and their growth needs.

For those who know me personally and who've worked with me professionally, I can see those grins creep across your faces because you know how passionate I am about training. For those of you who don't know me personally or professionally, one of the many roles I've held was Site Training Manager. Nothing infuriates me more than when a manager will not step up to the plate and take the time to invest in their people. It could be as simple as taking 5 minutes out of their day to do some on-the-job training because every little bit helps. But I will save this rant for another time, and step down from my soapbox now.

But remember—you can and should do everything in your power to create the right conditions for your team, but they still need to step up to the plate too. All the training in the world will mean nothing if the person is not willing to use it and do their best as well.

A star wants to see herself rise to the top. A leader wants to see those around her become stars.

Simon Sinek

Chapter 5: Getting the Work Done: Problem Solving

Clear is kind. Unclear is unkind.

Brené Brown

In any work environment, there are always goals, tasks, and targets to complete. Along with completing any goal, task, or target problems will undoubtedly arise. Keeping this in mind, what strategies can you follow to get the best from yourself and your team?

According to Quereto (2018), you will need to provide your team with clear direction so they can know when they have reached their destination. The most effective weapon to have in your arsenal is to have a strategy that will keep your team focused and motivated. One way to do this is to remind them what the goals are and how their efforts are contributing toward the bigger picture. When people start to feel that they are not adding value, they become discouraged and stagnant.

The direction to reach the goals you set should be clear and understandable; this sounds easier than it actually is. Dartnell (2014) provides the following guidelines to ensure your team understands your expectations and their purpose:

Don't assume they know what you mean. I have seen it happen too many times—managers go on a retreat or attend training and come back energized, full of new ideas, concepts, and information. They start throwing phrases and concepts around from the training and get upset when the team doesn't understand what they are supposed to do. They forget the team did not attend the same training. Your team might be the most skilled in the business, but they are definitely not mind readers. It's better to take a few minutes to explain clearly what you mean and need, rather than spending days or weeks trying to fix what went wrong because of a misunderstanding. And this doesn't have to come from training or retreat either, it could just as easily happen after a planning meeting or a war room session your team wasn't at.

Be clear and specific. Find the balance between saying too much and saying too little. People will lose interest if you don't get to the point quickly enough because you keep repeating yourself and trying to explain something they already understand the concept of – it begins to feel as though they're being talked down to. Or they may focus on the wrong points of whatever you are trying to convey. Be detailed and precise. Don't just say, "Order t-shirts for the team," if you have a specific t-shirt or design in mind. It's also a good idea to give examples, especially if it's an employee's first time doing a task. Just because what you are saying makes sense in your head, doesn't mean they are on the same page. So, make sure it's clear by asking them to explain it back to you.

Give time frames. Everybody loves to park the productivity train at the procrastination station, myself included, so set a due date. Otherwise, you will not end up where you need to be in time. An ambiguous phrase like 'soon' can mean a lot of different things to different people.

Give alternatives. There should never be alternatives to the goal, but the road to get there should have some flexibility. For example, if you're completing a project for a client and having a formal meeting with them, you should describe the goal but provide a range of due dates and options to get the project done.

Set boundaries. Your employees should be given clear boundaries for when they should come to you for further input and when they can solve problems on their own. You want them to be autonomous, but you also don't want them to struggle. Don't let people drown in confusion, going back and forth about whether to get you involved or not. On the other hand, they may know perfectly well what do to but because of past managers, they feel they have to run every decision by you. This has happened to me in the past. The resolution was as simple as letting my lead know which situations to decide on his own and if I ever felt it wasn't the decision I would have made, then we'd discuss it afterwards so moving forward our thinking and decision making would be in alignment with each other. We would take it as a learning opportunity. So, give them guidelines and coach them through situations by letting them know what those boundaries look like for you and you'll be helping to develop their autonomy in the process.

Get clarification. This step can be tricky at times. You don't want to embarrass or patronize your employees and you also want to avoid any potential misunderstandings. So, don't be afraid to ask them to repeat key instructions back to you, just to make sure they understand and feel prepared.

Best efforts are essential. Unfortunately, people charging this way and that way without guidance of principles can do a lot of damage.

W. Edwards Deming

Those tips should help keep the work going, but what happens when people just have a bad day? They overslept, their check engine light came on, their coffee spilled, and now they are struggling to make it through the day. What do you do then? In this situation, the only thing you can do is empathize. You've had bad days before; you know how it feels. Help them feel encouraged and heard. But what if empathy isn't your strongest suit? Don't worry; you can improve.

Building personal empathy isn't some sort of 5 step program, but there are a few things you can work on, and a few concepts to practice. First and foremost is truly listening, everyone wants and needs to feel heard; without this, you automatically fail. Next is to help people develop their self-confidence. Give them praise and recognition when they do well, and learn how to give positive and constructive feedback. There is also something to be said for the old adage of giving praise in public and feedback in private. For some, receiving feedback is no big deal and for others, it may feel like the end of the world at times so the more you know your people the more easily you can adapt to what suits them best. You always want to handle poor performance right away—don't let it fester, but don't dismantle the employee's confidence. Help them learn, and notice when they do it right next time. As you practice these, you'll build a rapport with your team, and you'll be more emotionally in tune with them, which is vital. We'll talk more about this a little later though.

On occasion, you may need to find ways to lift your employees out of a work rut when they no longer find joy and inspiration in their work or the people they work with. Once excitement disappears, people will focus on just getting through the day instead of going above and beyond the base requirements. You also may be the one that gets stuck in a rut, and you will need to find ways to keep yourself engaged within the workplace as well. Reach out to others when you feel stuck so you can continue to lead your team the way they need to be led. Don't be afraid to ask for help, this is what will make you an outstanding leader because we all struggle sometimes and this will show your team it's okay to admit you aren't perfect. Not only that, but that if you're struggling your most engaged employees will notice something is off. Now isn't the time to dawn your cape and pretend you are superhuman, save that for your kid's bedtime stories.

Stillman (2015) suggests these tips for keeping yourself and your team motivated:

Believe in the best of the team and yourself: Assume you will kick ass every time you walk into a room or begin a new project. Sometimes this means you will need to take a leap of faith by trusting an employee with a new task, but that is a good thing.

Make use of the resources around you: Don't just listen to the loudest person in the room, since an empty pot makes the most noise. Find ways to get contributions from the wallflowers as well. You'll learn quickly this may be where your best and brightest ideas come from.

Don't confuse idea generation with idea evaluation: When you're asking for suggestions, listen until all have been placed on the table. Only once everybody has had an opportunity to speak up do you start evaluating the merits of each idea.

Create a team full of people that can take over for you: This is a scary concept, and often a manager's fear will kick in at this stage. That's normal to an extent until you realize not only are your people your best assets but also a direct reflection of your leadership abilities. This is why it's necessary for your team become so well trained they can replace you, take over parts of your job, or do things well beyond your own capabilities. This is what you should always be striving for as a leader.

Check your bias at the door: Take time to understand and correct your own bias in order to avoid an atmosphere of favoritism. You will have some employees you naturally get along with better and stand out as outstanding employees, even so, it's the ones who need a little more support or the ones you don't get along with that you need to see and remove the bias from. They truly could be rockstars if you were just willing to give them a fair chance and help build them up. After all, that is your job.

An organization that follows these actions will have happy employees, and if you follow them as well, you will have a happier team.

> *The greatest waste in America is failure to use the abilities of people.*
>
> *W. Edwards Deming*

But your team won't be happy if they're constantly struggling to get resources. Though your team is your most important resource, they will still need other tangible goods and services to get the job done. This is, after all, one of your key responsibilities as a leader. A manager would shrug their shoulders and throw up their hands in defeat if they can't procure the resources their team so desperately needs. A leader will exhaust every option possible and keep looking for alternate solutions. Be a leader, your team will notice when you go to bat for them and when you don't.

By having spent time with your team, you will know what resources they need. If you don't, you haven't spent enough time with them or asked the right questions. Make sure your team has access to the critical elements they need without frustrating lag times.

If you employ well-balanced resource management within your department, you will soon see reduced costs, improved efficiency, efficacy, and better communication. These will improve team decision-making and increase the happiness of your team; by now you should understand how important this is! (Kltowska, 2020)

Resource scarcity can quickly result in conflict, so make sure the team has the basic resources they need to perform their tasks as effectively and efficiently as possible. Don't be bullied into buying "nice to haves" if your budget is tight. Always make sure they have the must-haves and they know how to use them.

LEADERSHIP VS. MANAGEMENT

You must also make sure your team is prepared for any situation. Whether it be your absence or an extreme budget cut, you need a team of problem solvers. If you want your team to be more efficient, they will need to be able to deal with problems if and when they arise. They may not always be personally equipped to deal with the problem itself though. Say they need an engineer or maintenance because they are a supervisor and don't possess that specific knowledge and skill set, make sure they know who their best contacts are to solve whatever issue pops up.

Knowing challenges will come up, how do you prepare your team for them? Luckily, it's not as complicated as you may think.

Make sure you hire the right people and trust them. You need people who are capable and independent. Make sure to give your employees space, otherwise, they will learn to rely on you being available to them at all times. Especially if they're used to you constantly looking over their shoulders. You don't have to be a helicopter manager to ensure the job gets done properly. Just check in with your team from time to time and make sure they are still on track in terms of delivering on their targets (7 ways, 2017).

Give your team goals, not instructions, and encourage creativity and brainstorming. Let them find their own path to the agreed destination, together. People tend to stew on problems for too long on their own, so get them into a habit of working together as a team to solve problems. Remember, you can't force people to think creatively, but you can turn your physical office space into an environment that fosters creativity by adding decor, such as plants or abstract art. Why? Because the ability to solve problems requires innovation and creativity. To put it simply, a team that can come up with new ideas is a team that can solve a problem (7 ways, 2017).

Appreciate new ideas. If you are constantly shooting down new ideas, people will become too scared to share and you may soon be missing out on a lot of awesome opportunities. People will get out of the habit of problem-solving if you are constantly breaking down their inputs and they are feeling criticized every time they are trying to help. Even if an idea isn't the best, you need to still discuss the pros and cons to respect it and the person who thought of it (7 ways, 2017).

When your team is proficient at their duties, trusted, appreciated, and has their creativity encouraged, they will have all the skills they need to survive any challenge.

A person and an organization must have goals, take actions to achieve those goals, gather evidence of achievement, study and reflect on the data and from that take actions again. Thus, they are in a continuous feedback spiral toward continuous improvement.

W. Edwards Deming

Chapter 6: Sheep vs. Shepherd: Creating Value in Your Organization

---

At well-led companies, people talk about the strength of the values. At poorly led companies, people complain about pay and benefits.

Simon Sinek

Ernest Shackleton was an Antarctic explorer who rose to prominence because one of his planned expeditions across Antarctica nearly ended in the death of the entire expedition team. Their ship became trapped in ice and they were stranded for nearly two years. Though it may seem odd at first, Ernest Shackleton can be viewed by many as a great example of leadership, despite the fact that his biggest success was a result of a monumental life-threatening failure.

But what made Shackleton a great leader? The simple fact that he understood his men. He knew their individual strengths and weaknesses, and how to motivate them. More than that, he put the welfare of his men above everything else and would never ask them to do anything he wasn't willing to do himself. Can you say the same? When in a tight spot he knew how to improvise and would abandon conventional behavior and his preconceived plans if they were no longer relevant to the situation.

On Shackleton's first expedition across the South Pole, he came within 97 miles of reaching his destination but turned around. Although his team might have had enough food to make it to the Pole, they did not have enough to make it safely back again. He chose the safety of his team members above the personal glory he would have received as the first expedition leader to reach the South Pole.

His leadership skills are best demonstrated by the fact that he managed to keep 28 men alive for nearly two years. While in the middle of a frozen wilderness with dwindling resources, he instilled a belief in his team that they would all make it safely back home. His message was simple and his goal even more so—safety and survival for all.

Smith (2020) provides the following insights regarding how he managed to pull off the unimaginable:

- To avoid the formation of cliques or conflicts, he insisted the men not spend longer than a week sharing a tent with the same men.

- He treated all men equally but took care of those who were struggling.

- Each person was made to believe they were important in contributing to the survival of the entire group.

- Scientists and sailors alike were required to do the same chores.

- Crew members were supplied with winter clothing before officers, and he even gave away his own gloves to a desperate colleague.

- Pessimism was never allowed to take root, the men were kept busy to avoid idleness which would inevitably lead them to contemplate their fate.

- Discipline was imposed with a light touch, but questioning of leadership was not tolerated.

- Routine was enforced despite nothing going to plan.

- He kept his men well fed and ensured that they still had fun and celebrated birthdays.

- He never let his own anxiety show in front of his men.

Shackleton was a shepherd, but he did not treat his men like sheep—he treated them like people, knowing their survival was his first and only priority. Together they agreed on the values that would form the foundation and would see them through to reach this goal.

According to Brown (2018), "...a value is a way of being or believing that we hold most important. Living into our values means that we do more than profess our values, we practice them. We walk our talk. We are clear about what we believe and hold important, and we take care that our intentions, words, thoughts, and behaviors align with those values."

We all have personal values but when setting values at an organizational level remember these will play a significant role in the culture and the climate of the organization. As a leader, your personal set of values will provide the roadmap for achieving your own personal goals. They will also affect how you behave, as well as how you make decisions in both personal and professional arenas of your life.

Over time we even start integrating different values into our mindset as we learn, grow, change, and evolve. When our personal core values align closely with our organization's core values, we find peace in our work. As a leader, it's possible to create an environment where your team starts adopting the core values of the organization as their own.

As wonderful as this is, a lot of organizations are still getting it wrong in trying to manage how employees interpret and adopt company values. Especially given where they may currently be in terms of Maslow's Hierarchy of Needs. Most already know or have heard of this hierarchy but a refresher never hurts. McLeod (2020) describes Maslow's Hierarchy as a motivational theory in psychology comprising of a five-tier model of human needs; this theory is often depicted as a pyramid. From the bottom of the pyramid moving up we have basic physiological human needs (food, water, air, etc.), safety, love and belonging, esteem, and self-actualization. Once your needs have been intrinsically met at a basic level, you will move on to meet needs at higher levels.

Luckily, if you are at the "self-actualized" level within the need hierarchy, you do not go back to the basic needs level if you missed lunch. What research has found is once your needs have been intrinsically met at a basic level, you will move on to the next level. Moving through the hierarchy is also not unidirectional, and can change on several occasions during the course of a person's life.

Let's look at a quick example to solidify how this works. Take organization X—one of their values is "celebrate success," which is supposed to bring a fun element into the workplace. Now, you as a manager know the value aims to actually create a less stressed and happier work environment. Your team is often chasing deadlines, so letting your hair down once in a while is good for employee morale. Because of this, the team decides to incorporate the company value by having a "Pizza Friday" whenever a big deadline is met—you order a few dozen pizzas, and everybody leaves work at three.

The office is a mess after every Pizza Friday and it's up to the janitors to get the office ready for the next day. There are at least five uneaten pizzas every time and the janitors are forced to throw them away because they were instructed to do so. Maybe not directly, but when they were hired, they were told that it is a company "value" not to steal anything purchased by the organization. The company bought the pizza therefore, it belongs to the company. Even though, if they could take the pizza home to their families, they would have to worry about two fewer meals a week! But for fear of getting fired they just chuck what is left in the trash. Even when entire pizzas are completely untouched.

If this pattern is repeated month after month, will the staff at different levels of the organization actually continue to have the same feeling about "celebrating success"? How will they be motivated to perform their jobs to the best of their ability given this disconnect?

If you truly want to create a value-based organization, all employees—regardless of their salary scale or job title—should be able to see the true meaning of the values up close and personal. If they don't, they won't be able to make a connection between your actions and values and start adopting organizational values into their everyday actions.

According to Sime (2019), values will help an organization build a reliable guide employees can use to orientate themselves. If a company's values are clear and consistent, the decisions made within will also be consistent. Why? Because if we break down any day to its bare bones, it will take the form of a decision tree; some decisions may be mundane like what to have for lunch, while others may be more complex. Regardless, your days are made up of decisions that eventually become the life you live. Most of these decisions are guided by the values you hold dear. So when we are able to weave the values of our company into our daily lives we hold them intrinsically in all situations we encounter.

Integrity will become one of the core characteristics of your business the more entrenched your people are in its values. Integrity means choosing what is right over what is comfortable. In practice, this means your team will make the decisions that are in line with the values, even if it ends up meaning more work for them at the end of the day.

Regardless of whether or not integrity is a core value of your business, you want your employees to operate with integrity. Bednarski (n.d) defines a business with integrity as one that operates in accordance with a strong moral code, where decisions are made guided by the organization's internal compass.

So once again—does your business make decisions that align with its values?

This isn't a question to be ignored; the value integrity brings to the business cannot be measured in mere financial terms alone. If you and your organization are consistent and forthright, you will never lack for business or employees, even during times of challenge.

There is always room for improvement when it comes to integrity, and Bednarski (n.d) provides a few tips here as well. The first step is to evaluate your own integrity. If this sounds like a huge task, then you have a lot of work to do. And this IS NOT a place to skimp. Once you figure out where you land with integrity, learn what integrity means to others, both inside and outside of your organization. While you need to learn from others it is a MUST to hire people whose integrity fits with your organization. If they are great at their job, but an unreliable sleaze in the eyes of your people and customers, you've just completely damaged your reputation. So be consistent, honest, and transparent; transparency is a vital part of integrity in an organization.

Transparency will transcend far beyond the occasional glimpse into the dealings of your business through the publishing of a fluff article or your annual reports. How can your organization be transparent? Simple. Be honest about your procurement and production processes. Be accessible to your clients and employees. And be honest about what something will cost or the service that you are delivering (Bednarski, n.d.). If you say you're going to do something, do it. Bottom line.

Is this level of transparency worth it?

It should be.

Transparency creates a relationship of trust between the organization and its stakeholders (both internal and external). It eliminates unfairness, inequality, and earns more feedback from your team, which improves decision making. When people feel they can trust you and that you are genuine with them, they *will* return the favor. This information you earn also improves innovation within your team, which will benefit your company tremendously (Lee, 2018).

If you can figure out the right values for you and your team by finding the best strategy to make them part of your everyday dealings, you will be able to create a workplace that your team will be excited about. They will look forward to coming to work. It will become a place where everybody is proud to be and never wants to leave no matter where they are in the organization. A place people want to retire from, which is unheard of these days.

When it comes to values, like with all things in business, your team will expect you to lead by example. You cannot expect them to live the values if you are not willing and able to do the same. If employees sense in any way that you have been hypocritical in your actions, it will result in disenchantment, disappointment, frustration, and anger.

Brown (2018) provides the following guidelines for creating an environment in which employees can more easily live into the values:

Define what your values are. You can't walk the talk until you know what the talk is. If you haven't spent time thinking about the values and identifying them, how do you know what is important to you? Don't try to make it complex—some organizations and people want to have 15 values emblazoned on the walls of their boardroom, but when push comes to shove, there are usually one or two core values that drive us. Get down to those.

Take values from BS to behavior. Take the time to translate values from ideals to behavior, and teach your staff the skills they need to perform their jobs in a way that aligns with the values. Once they know the values, hold them accountable to execute them. If staff can't action the values daily, they become meaningless cat posters. You know the kind — a kitten hanging onto a branch with the words "hang in there" in italics. Even kittens can become disgruntled and feral much like your employees.

Be open to feedback. No matter how hard we try, sometimes things will not work out the way we intended and that's okay! We need to be open to feedback from those around us who will call us on our bullshit. It's only when we have somebody brave enough to hold the mirror up for us that we see we won't always get it right, even as leaders. Because of this, we have to walk with empathy for others and self-compassion for ourselves in those moments when we fall short of the original intent. Remember, it's just another growth opportunity.

Being an organization that lives and leads its values also means that, on occasion, you and your team will need to have difficult conversations—and I don't just mean conversations about performance. I mean the conversations about privilege. Conversations about how different the workplace experience will be across genders, races, religious views, corporate hierarchy, etc. Anything, where there can be points of difference, will need to be talked about. You might not always have the answers when it comes to these elements, but you must be willing to listen and accept that there will be different experiences within the workplace due to the diversity of the people you will hire.

These conversations and situations will be hard. No two will be alike and unfortunately, there isn't a guidebook here. Let your gut guide you from one situation to the next. The one piece of advice I can give you is to have patience and empathy always.

Feeding people half-truths or bullshit to make them feel better (which is almost always about making ourselves feel more comfortable) is unkind.

Brené Brown

Conclusion

Write a new ending for yourself, for the people you're meant to serve and support, and for your culture.

Brené Brown

As a leader, your future legacy within the organization may be based on how well you were able to manage the operational output of your team. However, the impact you will have on the people around you will be much more important than any accolades or bonuses.

The operational part will be easy, as the main driving force behind the path you will take will be your ability to make decisions. Remember the following key steps, as recommended by Onley (2019), for decision making:

- Set a deadline by when a decision should be made.

- Gather as many options as you possibly can. The last thing you want is to be forced into an unfavorable decision because you thought no other options were available to you.

- Imagine the worst that could happen for each option available and determine which of those you will prefer to deal with.

- Make decisions in line with your values.

- Remember that if you decide not to decide, you have effectively also made a decision.

- Make sure you understand the legal implications of your decisions.

The interpersonal aspect of your journey as a leader will be a lot more difficult to map and even more difficult to execute. You will need to not only manage your own heart and mind but help guide every team member that may cross your path along the way. You will need to build and maintain a relationship with yourself and your team. Knowing yourself is as important as knowing your team–maybe even more so since they will emulate what you put forth. To put it simply, if you don't like what you see in your team, take a good hard look at yourself and your actions because it all starts with you.

Relationships will die if there is no trust, so show your people you trust them and they will start trusting you. Treat them as the valuable resources they are and they will become valuable resources for you.

For you to become the leader you were meant to be, a lot of introspection will be required. You will never be the perfect leader because the perfect leader doesn't exist. We are people which means we are fallible and that's okay. As long as you know your weaknesses and put the effort in to address them, you will always be taking steps towards where you were meant to be.

Regardless of where your leadership journey may take you and with whom your paths may cross, always carry these six elements of Shackleton's leadership with you (Climer, 2016):

Model and inspire optimism. Emotions are contagious, so choose to spread optimism.

Develop a clear and shared purpose. Clarity of purpose is one of the most significant predictive factors for success.

Build unity and commitment within the team. Intentionally foster the values you want the team to ascribe to, but make sure unity and commitment to the cause feature high on the list.

Prioritize well-being. Without the team, you will never reach the goal—if your team is doing and feeling well, your goal will always be in reach.

Plan, but adapt. Have a plan and an alternate plan, but be ready to adapt when the circumstances require it. When things do not go according to plan, it is far easier to change the plan than it is to change the circumstances.

Make tough decisions. Along the way, tough decisions will need to be made that will make some people unhappy. Build relationships so alignment will not be lost in the aftermath of a tough decision. When a tough decision needs to be made, it's your job to make sure it has the best interests of the team in mind.

To leave you with one final thought:

Be the leader you wish you had.

Simon Sinek

References

7 Ways to Help Your Employees Become Better Problem-Solvers. (2017, March 23). Entrepreneur. https://www.entrepreneur.com/article/290752[1]

18 Reasons Why a Daily Routine Is So Important -. (2016, May 27). https://www.skilledatlife.com/18-reasons-why-a-daily-routine-is-so-important/[2]

A Step By Step Approach to Determine Your Return on Training Investment. (2016, December 16). Go2HR. https://www.go2hr.ca/training-development/roi-of-training/a-step-by-step-approach-to-determine-your-return-on-training-investment[3]

Anderson, M. (2017, July 19). *Leadership Demands Purpose: Lessons from Malala | On Leadership.* Buffalo.edu. https://ubwp.buffalo.edu/school-of-management-leadership/2017/07/19/leadership-demands-purpose-lessons-from-malala/[4]

Bartlett, B. (2018, February 2). *The main purpose of a coach |.* https://benmbartlett.com/the-main-purpose-of-a-coach/#:~:text=The%20main%20purpose%20of%20the%20coach%5

Bednarski, D. (n.d). *The Importance of Integrity in Business | FreshBooks Blog*. FreshBooks Blog - Resources & Advice for Small Business Owners. https://www.freshbooks.com/blog/integrity-in-business-why-its-important[6]

Britannica, T. Editors of Encyclopaedia (2021, February 12). *Ernest Shackleton. Encyclopedia Britannica*. https://www.britannica.com/biography/Ernest-Henry-Shackleton

Brown, Brene. (2010). *The gifts of imperfection: let go of who you think you're supposed to be and embrace who you are*. Hazelden.

Brown, Brene. (2012). *Daring greatly: how the courage to be vulnerable transforms the way we live, love, parent, and lead*. Gotham Books.

Brown, Brene. (2018). *Dare to Lead: Brave Work. Tough Conversations. Whole Hearts*. Ebury Publishing.

---

5. https://benmbartlett.com/the-main-purpose-of-a-coach/#_853ae90f0351324bd73ea615e6487517__4c761f170e016836ff84498202b99827__853ae90f0351324bd73ea615e6487517_text_43ec3e5dee6e706af7766fffea512721_The_0bcef9c45bd8a48eda1b26eb0c61c869_20main_0bcef9c45bd8a48eda1b26eb0c61c869_20purpose_0bcef9c45bd8a48eda1b26eb0c61c869_20of_0bcef9c45bd8a48eda1b26eb0c61c869_20the_0bcef9c45bd8a48eda1b26eb0c61c869_20coach_0bcef9c45bd8a48eda1b26eb0c61c869_20is_0bcef9c45bd8a48eda1b26eb0c61c869_20to_0bcef9c45bd8a48eda1b26eb0c61c869_20improve_0bcef9c45bd8a48eda1b26eb0c61c869_20performance

6. https://www.freshbooks.com/blog/integrity-in-business-why-its-important

Buschman, M. (2020, July 17). *Managing Dysfunctional Teams: How to Address Underlying Issues.* Training Industry. https://trainingindustry.com/articles/performance-management/dealing-with-dysfunctional-teams-how-to-address-underlying-issues/[7]

CFI. (2019). *Maslow's Hierarchy of Needs - Overview, Explanation, and Examples.* Corporate Finance Institute. https://corporatefinanceinstitute.com/resources/knowledge/other/maslows-hierarchy-of-needs/[8]

Cherry, K. (2020, June 3). *Overview of Emotional Intelligence.* Verywell Mind; Verywellmind. https://www.verywellmind.com/what-is-emotional-intelligence-2795423[9]

Clarke, J. (2020, September 17). *Want to Be More Productive and Confident? Develop a Morning Routine.* Verywell Mind. https://www.verywellmind.com/morning-routine-4174576#:~:text=The%20morning%20routine%20hel
[10]

---

7. https://trainingindustry.com/articles/performance-management/dealing-with-dysfunctional-teams-how-to-address-underlying-issues/
8. https://corporatefinanceinstitute.com/resources/knowledge/other/maslows-hierarchy-of-needs/
9. https://www.verywellmind.com/what-is-emotional-intelligence-2795423
10. https://www.verywellmind.com/morning-routine-4174576#_853ae90f0351324bd73ea615e6487517__4c761f170e016836ff84498202b99827__853ae90f0351324bd73ea615e6487517_text_43ec3e5dee6e706af7766fffea512721_The_0bcef9c45bd8a48eda1b26eb0c61c869_20morning_0bcef9c45bd8a48eda1b26eb0c61c869_20routine_0bcef9c45bd8a48eda1b26eb0c61c869_20helps_0bcef9c45bd8a48eda1b26eb0c61c869_20us

Clarke, S. (2018, May 15). *Why Your Values Are Key To Your Leadership | Leaderonomics.* Www.leaderonomics.com. https://www.leaderonomics.com/articles/leadership/values-key-leadership[11]

Climer, A. (2016, December 16). *Five Elements of Shackleton's Leadership.* Dr. Amy Climer. https://climerconsulting.com/five-elements-shackletons-leadership/[12]

Core Values of a Great Leader. (n.d.). Indeed Career Guide. https://www.indeed.com/career-advice/career-development/leadership-values#:~:text=Leadership%20values%20are%20importa
[13]

Dartnell, A. (2014, October 16). *7 tips on how to give clear, understandable instructions to staff.* Lifehack. https://www.lifehack.org/articles/work/7-tips-how-give-clear-understandable-instructions-staff.html[14]

Daskal, L. (2012, December 4). *Learn From Others - Lolly Daskal | Leadership.* Lolly Daskal.

---

11. https://www.leaderonomics.com/articles/leadership/values-key-leadership

12. https://climerconsulting.com/five-elements-shackletons-leadership/

13. https://www.indeed.com/career-advice/career-development/leadership-values#_853ae90f0351324bd73ea615e6487517__4c761f170e016836ff84498202b9 9827__853ae90f0351324bd73ea615e6487517_text_43ec3e5dee6e706af7766fffea512721_Lea dership_0bcef9c45bd8a48eda1b26eb0c61c869_20values_0bcef9c45bd8a48eda1b26eb0c61c86 9_20are_0bcef9c45bd8a48eda1b26eb0c61c869_20important_0bcef9c45bd8a48eda1b26eb0c6 1c869_20because

14. https://www.lifehack.org/articles/work/7-tips-how-give-clear-understandable-instructions-staff.html

https://www.lollydaskal.com/leadership/learn-from-others/[15]

Daskal, L. (2017, February 5). *12 Signs You Have the Mindset to Be a Great Leader - Lolly Daskal | Leadership*. Lolly Daskal. https://www.lollydaskal.com/leadership/12-signs-mindset-great-leader/[16]

Deering, S. (2019, January 4). *Top 7 Qualities of a Successful Team*. Undercover Recruiter. https://theundercoverrecruiter.com/qualities-successful-work-team/[17]

Editorial Staff. (2020, October 14). *Things To Learn From Malala Yousafzai's Unique Leadership*. Vision, Belief, Change. https://vbchange.com/malala-yousafzai/[18]

Five Tips On How To Manage Dysfunctional Teams. (2019, November 11). Nexecute Group. https://nexecutegroup.com/2019/11/five-tips-how-to-manage-dysfunctional-teams/[19]

Forbes Coaches Council. (2016, August 26). Council Post: 14 Warning Signs That Your Team Is Nearing Dysfunction. Forbes Coaches Council. https://www.forbes.com/sites/forbescoachescouncil/2016/08/26/14-warning-signs-that-your-team-is-nearing-dysfunction/?sh=1fabbca36bd5[20]

---

15. https://www.lollydaskal.com/leadership/learn-from-others/
16. https://www.lollydaskal.com/leadership/12-signs-mindset-great-leader/
17. https://theundercoverrecruiter.com/qualities-successful-work-team/
18. https://vbchange.com/malala-yousafzai/
19. https://nexecutegroup.com/2019/11/five-tips-how-to-manage-dysfunctional-teams/

Gallaher, L. (2021, January 14). *There's a dark side to looking on the bright side. Here's a healthier antidote.* Fast Company. https://www.fastcompany.com/90593972/theres-a-dark-side-to-looking-on-the-bright-side-heres-a-healthier-antidote[21]

Gallo, A. (2011, February 7). *Making Sure Your Employees Succeed.* Harvard Business Review. https://hbr.org/2011/02/making-sure-your-employees-suc[22]

Gavin, M. (2020, March 24). *Decision-Making in Management: 5 Common Pitfalls to Avoid | HBS Online.* Business Insights - Blog. https://online.hbs.edu/blog/post/decision-making-in-management[23]

Get a Dysfunctional Team Back on Track. (2015, March 30). Harvard Business Review. https://hbr.org/2013/11/get-a-dysfunctional-team-back-on-track[24]

Gibbs, A. (2018, January 31). *Malala Yousafzai: Anyone can bring about change at any point — and at any age.* CNBC; CNBC. https://www.cnbc.com/2018/01/31/malala-yousafzai-on-leadership-and-her-own-career-path.html[25]

---

20. https://www.forbes.com/sites/forbescoachescouncil/2016/08/26/14-warning-signs-that-your-team-is-nearing-dysfunction/?sh=1fabbca36bd5
21. https://www.fastcompany.com/90593972/theres-a-dark-side-to-looking-on-the-bright-side-heres-a-healthier-antidote
22. https://hbr.org/2011/02/making-sure-your-employees-suc
23. https://online.hbs.edu/blog/post/decision-making-in-management
24. https://hbr.org/2013/11/get-a-dysfunctional-team-back-on-track
25. https://www.cnbc.com/2018/01/31/malala-yousafzai-on-leadership-and-her-own-career-path.html

Gladwell, M. (2008). *Outliers: the story of success*. Back Bay Books, Cop.

Gottfredson, R., & Reina, C. (2020, January 17). *To Be a Great Leader, You Need the Right Mindset*. Harvard Business Review. https://hbr.org/2020/01/to-be-a-great-leader-you-need-the-right-mindset[26]

Grylls, Bear. (2016). *A survival guide for life: how to achieve your goals, thrive in adversity and grow in character*. Corgi Books.

Holton, L. (2020, June 4). *10 Science-Backed Benefits of a Morning Routine*. MYVA360. https://myva360.com/blog/10-science-backed-benefits-of-a-morning-routine[27]

Ivy Exec. (2021, March 1). *Could You Be Spreading Toxic Positivity to Your Team?* Ivy Exec Blog. https://www.ivyexec.com/career-advice/2021/could-you-be-spreading-toxic-positivity-to-your-team/#:~:text=Another%20concern%20with%20toxic%20positivity[28]

Kltowska, A. (2020, May 26). *Why is Resource Management Important? How Can You Benefit From It?* Teamdeck.io.

---

26. https://hbr.org/2020/01/to-be-a-great-leader-you-need-the-right-mindset
27. https://myva360.com/blog/10-science-backed-benefits-of-a-morning-routine
28. https://www.ivyexec.com/career-advice/2021/could-you-be-spreading-toxic-positivity-to-your-team/#_853ae90f0351324bd73ea615e6487517__4c761f170e016836ff84498202b99827__85 3ae90f0351324bd73ea615e6487517_text_43ec3e5dee6e706af7766fffea512721_Another_0bc ef9c45bd8a48eda1b26eb0c61c869_20concern_0bcef9c45bd8a48eda1b26eb0c61c869_20with _0bcef9c45bd8a48eda1b26eb0c61c869_20toxic_0bcef9c45bd8a48eda1b26eb0c61c869_20pos itivity

https://teamdeck.io/leadership/is-resource-management-important/[29]

Kruse, K. (2013, April 9). *What Is Leadership?* Forbes. https://www.forbes.com/sites/kevinkruse/2013/04/09/what-is-leadership/?sh=5661c16c5b90[30]

Landry, L. (2020, March 5). *Why Managers Should Involve Their Team in Decision-Making | HBS Online.* Business Insights - Blog. https://online.hbs.edu/blog/post/team-decision-making[31]

Lee, K. (2018, October 29). *Why Business Transparency Matters (and How to Get Started).* Buffer Resources. https://buffer.com/resources/transparency-in-business/[32]

Lumen. (2019). *Defining Teams and Teamwork | Boundless Management.* Lumenlearning.com. https://courses.lumenlearning.com/boundless-management/chapter/defining-teams-and-teamwork/[33]

Madhusudan, P. (2019, March 7). *One man who inspired the world - Mahatma Gandhi & his leadership value.* People Matters. https://www.peoplemattersglobal.com/article/leadership/one-man-who-inspired-the-world-mahatma-gandhi-his-leadership-value-16500[34]

---

29. https://teamdeck.io/leadership/is-resource-management-important/
30. https://www.forbes.com/sites/kevinkruse/2013/04/09/what-is-leadership/?sh=5661c16c5b90
31. https://online.hbs.edu/blog/post/team-decision-making
32. https://buffer.com/resources/transparency-in-business/
33. https://courses.lumenlearning.com/boundless-management/chapter/defining-teams-and-teamwork/

Manktelow, J., & Birkinshaw, J. (2018, June 12). *HR Magazine - How to get the best out of your team*. HR Magazine. https://www.hrmagazine.co.uk/content/features/how-to-get-the-best-out-of-your-team[35]

Martin, K. (2019, August 7). *HR Magazine - How to lift your top team out of a work rut*. HR Magazine. https://www.hrmagazine.co.uk/content/features/how-to-lift-your-top-team-out-of-a-work-rut[36]

Martinuzzi, B. (2018). *Leading by Example: How to Lead a Team Honestly and Authentically*. Mindtools.com. https://www.mindtools.com/pages/article/newLDR_60.htm[37]

Mcleod, S. (2020, December 29). *Maslow's Hierarchy of Needs*. Simply Psychology. https://www.simplypsychology.org/maslow.html#gsc.tab=0[38]

Melnyck, R. (2019, September 17). *Why It's Important to Learn from Others and How to Do It*. Prime Your Pump. https://primeyourpump.com/2019/09/17/learn-from-others/[39]

---

34. https://www.peoplemattersglobal.com/article/leadership/one-man-who-inspired-the-world-mahatma-gandhi-his-leadership-value-16500
35. https://www.hrmagazine.co.uk/content/features/how-to-get-the-best-out-of-your-team
36. https://www.hrmagazine.co.uk/content/features/how-to-lift-your-top-team-out-of-a-work-rut
37. https://www.mindtools.com/pages/article/newLDR_60.htm
38. https://www.simplypsychology.org/maslow.html#gsc.tab_43ec3e5dee6e706af7766fffea512721_0
39. https://primeyourpump.com/2019/09/17/learn-from-others/

Miguel, M. (2018, May 7). *Define Friend: A Good Understanding Of The Friend Definition | Betterhelp.* Betterhelp.com; BetterHelp. https://www.betterhelp.com/advice/friendship/define-friend-a-good-understanding-of-the-friend-definition/[40]

Miller, K. (2020, March 19). *5 Critical Steps in the Change Management Process | HBS Online.* Business Insights - Blog. https://online.hbs.edu/blog/post/change-management-process[41]

Mindtools. (2009). *Mintzberg's Management RolesIdentifying the Roles Managers Play.* Mindtools.com. https://www.mindtools.com/pages/article/management-roles.htm[42]

Nayar, V. (2014, August 7). *Three Differences Between Managers and Leaders.* Harvard Business Review. https://hbr.org/2013/08/tests-of-a-leadership-transiti[43]

Onley, D. (2019, August 29). *How Leaders Can Make Better Decisions.* SHRM; SHRM. https://www.shrm.org/hr-today/news/hr-magazine/fall2019/pages/how-leaders-can-make-better-decisions.aspx[44]

---

40. https://www.betterhelp.com/advice/friendship/define-friend-a-good-understanding-of-the-friend-definition/
41. https://online.hbs.edu/blog/post/change-management-process
42. https://www.mindtools.com/pages/article/management-roles.htm
43. https://hbr.org/2013/08/tests-of-a-leadership-transiti
44. https://www.shrm.org/hr-today/news/hr-magazine/fall2019/pages/how-leaders-can-make-better-decisions.aspx

Pariona, A. (2017, June 2). *How Fear Is Deep-Rooted in Our Everyday Life and Controlling Us*. Lifehack; Lifehack. https://www.lifehack.org/596645/how-fear-is-deep-rooted-in-our-everyday-life-and-controlling-us[45]

Quereto, J. (2018, March 20). *Eight Best Practices of Change: Clear Direction*. Expressworks International. https://www.expressworks.com/change-leadership-capability/eight-best-practices-of-change-clear-direction/[46]

Reh, F. J. (2020, January 17). *Here's the Positive Trait That Makes a Great Leader and Manager*. The Balance Careers. https://www.thebalancecareers.com/leaders-are-always-positive-2275805#:~:text=Great%20leaders%20are%20always%20positive [47]

Riggio, R. (2013). *Characteristics of Good Work Team Members*. Psychology Today. https://www.psychologytoday.com/us/blog/cutting-edge-leadership/201301/characteristics-good-work-team-members[48]

---

45. https://www.lifehack.org/596645/how-fear-is-deep-rooted-in-our-everyday-life-and-controlling-us

46. https://www.expressworks.com/change-leadership-capability/eight-best-practices-of-change-clear-direction/

47. https://www.thebalancecareers.com/leaders-are-always-positive-2275805#_853ae90f0351324bd73ea615e6487517__4c761f170e016836ff84498202b99827__853ae90f0351324bd73ea615e6487517_text_43ec3e5dee6e706af7766fffea512721_Great_0bcef9c45bd8a48eda1b26eb0c61c869_20leaders_0bcef9c45bd8a48eda1b26eb0c61c869_20are_0bcef9c45bd8a48eda1b26eb0c61c869_20always_0bcef9c45bd8a48eda1b26eb0c61c869_20positive

Roberts, J. (2019, June 26). *Predictable Success: Creating Routine to Strengthen Your Team*. Difference Consulting. https://differenceconsulting.com/blog/predictable-success-creating-routine-strengthen-team/[49]

Role of the Coach. (n.d.). Www.topendsports.com. Retrieved April 4, 2021, from https://www.topendsports.com/fitness/coach.htm#:~:text=Sports%20coaches%20assist%20athletes%20in [50]

Schrage, M. (2016, October 5). *Like it or not, you are always leading by example*. https://hbr.org/2016/10/like-it-or-not-you-are-always-leading-by-example[51]

Schwartzberg, J. (2016, February 29). *Why You Shouldn't "Friend" Your Employees*. Mediabistro. https://www.mediabistro.com/climb-the-ladder/managing/why-you-shouldnt-friend-your-

---

48. https://www.psychologytoday.com/us/blog/cutting-edge-leadership/201301/characteristics-good-work-team-members
49. https://differenceconsulting.com/blog/predictable-success-creating-routine-strengthen-team/
50. https://www.topendsports.com/fitness/coach.htm#_853ae90f0351324bd73ea615e6487517__4c761f170e016836ff84498202b99827__853ae90f0351324bd73ea615e6487517_text_43ec3e5dee6e706af7766fffea512721_Sports_0b cef9c45bd8a48eda1b26eb0c61c869_20coaches_0bcef9c45bd8a48eda1b26eb0c61c869_20assis t_0bcef9c45bd8a48eda1b26eb0c61c869_20athletes_0bcef9c45bd8a48eda1b26eb0c61c869_2 0in
51. https://hbr.org/2016/10/like-it-or-not-you-are-always-leading-by-example

employees/#:~:text=Being%20too%20friendly%20can%20jeopardize [52]

Scivicque, C. (2019, April 16). *The Benefits of Workplace Routines and How to Set Them Up*. Eat Your Career. https://eatyourcareer.com/2019/04/the-benefits-of-workplace-routines-and-how-to-set-them-up/ [53]

Scully, D. (2018, August 7). *The 5 stages of team development*. Www.teamwork.com. https://www.teamwork.com/blog/the-5-stages-of-team-development-what-you-need-to-know/ [54]

Sime, C. (2019a, January 25). *Please Get To Know Your Values*. Forbes. https://www.forbes.com/sites/carleysime/2019/01/25/please-get-to-know-your-values/?sh=2dbe1bfb49d2 [55]

Sime, C. (2019b, February 15). *The Power Of Values In Leadership*. Forbes. https://www.forbes.com/sites/carleysime/2019/02/15/the-power-of-values-in-leadership/?sh=70dd58b06f76 [56]

---

52. https://www.mediabistro.com/climb-the-ladder/managing/why-you-shouldnt-friend-your-employees/#_853ae90f0351324bd73ea615e6487517__4c761f170e016836ff84498202b99827__853ae90f0351324bd73ea615e6487517_text_43ec3e5dee6e706af7766fffea512721_Being_0bcef9c45bd8a48eda1b26eb0c61c869_20too_0bcef9c45bd8a48eda1b26eb0c61c869_20friendly_0bcef9c45bd8a48eda1b26eb0c61c869_20can_0bcef9c45bd8a48eda1b26eb0c61c869_20jeopardize

53. https://eatyourcareer.com/2019/04/the-benefits-of-workplace-routines-and-how-to-set-them-up/

54. https://www.teamwork.com/blog/the-5-stages-of-team-development-what-you-need-to-know/

55. https://www.forbes.com/sites/carleysime/2019/01/25/please-get-to-know-your-values/?sh=2dbe1bfb49d2

Sinek, S. (2017). *Leaders eat last: why some teams pull together and others don't.* Portfolio/Penguin, An Imprint Of Penguin Random House Llc.

Smith, M. (n.d.). *What made Shackleton a great leader?* Shackleton. Retrieved April 4, 2021, from https://shackletonlondon.com/blogs/articles/shackleton-great-leader#:~:text=Shackleton[57]

Stillman, J. (2015, July 20). *5 Unexpected Ideas to Get the Best Out of Your Team.* Inc.com; Inc. https://www.inc.com/jessica-stillman/5-unexpected-ideas-to-get-the-best-out-of-your-team.html[58]

The 5-Step Process to Defining Authentic Leadership. (2020, January 7). The Leadership Institute. https://www.theleadershipinstitute.com.au/2020/01/5-steps-to-defining-your-authentic-leadership/[59]

The Importance of a Positive Attitude for Team Leaders. (2015, June 25). TBAE Team Building Blog. https://www.tbae.co.za/blog/the-importance-of-a-positive-attitude-for-team-leaders/[60]

---

56. https://www.forbes.com/sites/carleysime/2019/02/15/the-power-of-values-in-leadership/?sh=70dd58b06f76

57. https://shackletonlondon.com/blogs/articles/shackleton-great-leader#_853ae90f0351324bd73ea615e6487517__4c761f170e016836ff84498 202b99827__853ae90f0351324bd73ea615e6487517_text_43ec3e5dee6e706af7766fffea51272 1_Shackleton

58. https://www.inc.com/jessica-stillman/5-unexpected-ideas-to-get-the-best-out-of-your-team.html

59. https://www.theleadershipinstitute.com.au/2020/01/5-steps-to-defining-your-authentic-leadership/

The Importance of Training and Development in the Workplace. (n.d.). 2020 Project Management. https://2020projectmanagement.com/resources/project-management-training-and-qualifications/the-importance-of-training-and-development-in-the-workplace#:~:text=A%20training%20program%20allows%20you [61]

The Importance of Training Employees: 11 Benefits. (n.d.). Indeed Career Guide. Retrieved April 4, 2021, from https://www.indeed.com/career-advice/career-development/importance-of-training#:~:text=It%20improves%20skills%20and%20kn [62]

The Leadership Institute. (2020, January 7). *The 5-Step Process to Defining Authentic Leadership.* The Leadership Institute. https://www.theleadershipinstitute.com.au/2020/01/5-steps-to-defining-your-authentic-leadership/ [63]

---

60. https://www.tbae.co.za/blog/the-importance-of-a-positive-attitude-for-team-leaders/

61. https://2020projectmanagement.com/resources/project-management-training-and-qualifications/the-importance-of-training-and-development-in-the-workplace#_853ae90f0351324bd73ea615e6487517__4c761f170e016836ff84498202b99827__853ae90f0351324bd73ea615e6487517_text_43ec3e5dee6e706af7766fffea512721_A_0bcef9c45bd8a48eda1b26eb0c61c869_20training_0bcef9c45bd8a48eda1b26eb0c61c869_20program_0bcef9c45bd8a48eda1b26eb0c61c869_20allows_0bcef9c45bd8a48eda1b26eb0c61c869_20you

62. https://www.indeed.com/career-advice/career-development/importance-of-training#_853ae90f0351324bd73ea615e6487517__4c761f170e016836ff84498202b99827__853ae90f0351324bd73ea615e6487517_text_43ec3e5dee6e706af7766fffea512721_It_0bcef9c45bd8a48eda1b26eb0c61c869_20improves_0bcef9c45bd8a48eda1b26eb0c61c869_20skills_0bcef9c45bd8a48eda1b26eb0c61c869_20and_0bcef9c45bd8a48eda1b26eb0c61c869_20knowledge

Torres, M. (2020, December 3). *5 Signs You're Experiencing Toxic Positivity At Work*. HuffPost. https://www.huffpost.com/entry/signs-experiencing-toxic-positivity-at-work_l_5fc7cedcc5b640945e52ce30[64]

Valdez, L. (2020, January 2). *Are You Coachable? And, Why Does It Matter?* American Academy of Estate Planning Attorneys. https://www.aaepa.com/2020/01/are-you-coachable-and-why-does-it-matter/#:~:text=If%20you[65]

Vrabie, A. (2014, May 23). *Are routines good for your team productivity?* Sandglaz Blog Archive. https://blog.sandglaz.com/routines-good-team-productivity/[66]

Ward, S. (2020, September 17). *Leadership Definition*. The Balance Small Business; The Balance. https://www.thebalancesmb.com/leadership-definition-2948275[67]

What Qualities Made Gandhi a Good Leader? (n.d.). Reference.com. Retrieved April 4, 2021, from https://www.reference.com/world-view/qualities-made-

---

63. https://www.theleadershipinstitute.com.au/2020/01/5-steps-to-defining-your-authentic-leadership/

64. https://www.huffpost.com/entry/signs-experiencing-toxic-positivity-at-work_l_5fc7cedcc5b640945e52ce30

65. https://www.aaepa.com/2020/01/are-you-coachable-and-why-does-it-matter/#_853ae90f0351324bd73ea615e6487517__4c761f170e016836ff84498202b99827__853ae90f0351324bd73ea615e6487517_text_43ec3e5dee6e706af7766fffea512721_If_0bcef9c45bd8a48eda1b26eb0c61c869_20you

66. https://blog.sandglaz.com/routines-good-team-productivity/

67. https://www.thebalancesmb.com/leadership-definition-2948275

gandhi-good-leader-
e8d2d3089f510959#:~:text=Qualities%20that%20made%20Gandhi%2
68

Wikipedia Contributors. (2019, January 14). *Malala Yousafzai*. Wikipedia; Wikimedia Foundation. https://en.wikipedia.org/wiki/Malala_Yousafzai[69]

Winterhalter, K. (2016, September 12). *Teamwork makes the Dreamwork—Not!* Insight Assessment. https://www.insightassessment.com/blog/teamwork-makes-the-dreamwork-not[70]

Winterhalter, K. (2020, January 16). *5 Decision Making Skills for Successful Leaders*. Insight Assessment. https://www.insightassessment.com/blog/5-decision-making-skills-for-successful-leaders[71]

---

68. https://www.reference.com/world-view/qualities-made-gandhi-good-leader-e8d2d3089f510959#_853ae90f0351324bd73ea615e6487517__4c761f170e016836ff84498202b99827__853ae90f0351324bd73ea615e6487517_text_43ec3e5dee6e706af7766fffea512721_Qualities_0bcef9c45bd8a48eda1b26eb0c61c869_20that_0bcef9c45bd8a48eda1b26eb0c61c869_20made_0bcef9c45bd8a48eda1b26eb0c61c869_20Gandhi_0bcef9c45bd8a48eda1b26eb0c61c869_20a

69. https://en.wikipedia.org/wiki/Malala_Yousafzai

70. https://www.insightassessment.com/blog/teamwork-makes-the-dreamwork-not

71. https://www.insightassessment.com/blog/5-decision-making-skills-for-successful-leaders

Don't miss out!

Visit the website below and you can sign up to receive emails whenever Mowgli J. Bear publishes a new book. There's no charge and no obligation.

https://books2read.com/r/B-A-BFKQ-QNLSB

BOOKS2READ

Connecting independent readers to independent writers.

www.ingramcontent.com/pod-product-compliance
Lightning Source LLC
Chambersburg PA
CBHW020206090426
42734CB00008B/960